PREFACE

We are pleased to present this comprehensive collection of **CBSE Data Science Class 10 Solved Papers**, compiled under subject code **419**. These papers have been carefully selected and solved to provide students with a clear understanding of the pattern, types of questions, and the marking scheme used in the CBSE Board examinations.

Data Science, being a relatively new and rapidly evolving field, demands a strong foundation in both theoretical knowledge and practical application. The papers included in this book are designed to help students develop a deep understanding of the subject matter and build the necessary skills to tackle the challenges posed by the board exams.

Features of This Book:
Authentic CBSE Board Papers: The book contains the actual question papers from the CBSE board exam, ensuring that students have access to the most relevant and up-to-date material.
Detailed Solutions: Each question is accompanied by a step-by-step solution, providing clear explanations and justifications for the answers. This not only helps in understanding the correct approach but also aids in learning how to effectively present answers in the exam.
Marking Scheme Analysis: The solutions are aligned with the official CBSE marking scheme, offering insights into how marks are distributed for each type of question. This helps students prioritize their preparation and focus on the areas that carry the most weight.
Exam Strategy Tips: Throughout the book, students will find tips and strategies for managing time, avoiding common mistakes, and maximizing their scores. These tips are derived from the analysis of previous years' papers and are aimed at helping students perform their best on exam day.
Comprehensive Coverage: The book covers all key topics within the Data Science syllabus, ensuring that students are well-prepared for any question that may appear on the exam.

We believe that this book will be an invaluable resource for Class 10 students as they prepare for their Data Science board exams. By working through these solved papers, students will gain the confidence and skills needed to excel in their exams and lay a strong foundation for further studies in Data Science and related fields.
We wish all students the best of luck in their exams and hope that this book serves as a useful tool in their academic journey.

Table of Contents

CBSE Previous Year Solved Question Paper 2023

SUBJECT CODE: 419

SET-4

Q.P. CODE: 106

Instructions:

Please check that this question paper contains **21** questions.

Q.P. Code given on the right-hand side of the question paper should be written on the title page of the answer-book by the candidate.

Please write down the serial number of the question in the answer-book before attempting it.

15-minute time has been allotted to read this question paper. The question paper will be distributed at 10.15 a.m. From 10.15 a.m. to 10.30 a.m., the students will read the question paper only and will not write any answer on the answer-book during this period.

DATA SCIENCE

Time allowed: 2 hours

Maximum Marks: 50

General Instructions:

1. Please read the instructions carefully.
2. This question paper consists of 21 questions in two sections: Section A and Section B.
3. Section A has Objective Type Questions, whereas Section B contains Subjective Type Questions.
4. Out of the given (5 + 16 =) 21 questions, the candidate has to answer (5 + 10 =) 15 questions in the allotted (maximum) time of 2 hours.
5. All questions of a particular section must be attempted in the correct order.
6. Section A: Objective Type Questions (24 marks):
    a. This section has 5 questions.
    b. There is no negative marking.

c. Do as per the instructions given.

d. Marks allotted are mentioned against each question/part.

7. Section B: Subjective Type Questions (26 marks):

a. This section has 16 questions.

b. A candidate has to do 10 questions.

c. Do as per the instructions given.

d. Marks allotted are mentioned against each question/part.

SECTION A

(Objective Type Questions) (24 marks)

1. Answer any 4 out of the given 6 questions on Employability Skills. (4X1=4)

(i) Stress management can help you to

a. have a joyful life.

b. have a stressful life.

c. be less energetic.

d. have no time for friends and family.

Answer: a

Reason: Stress management techniques help reduce stress, leading to a more balanced and joyful life. Proper stress management improves mental and physical health, allowing individuals to enjoy life more fully.

(ii) Which type of motivation makes us do things because they make us happy?

a. Internal motivation

b. External motivation

c. Both (a) and (b)

d. Neither (a) nor (b)

Answer: a

Reason: Internal motivation refers to doing something because it is inherently satisfying or enjoyable. This type of motivation comes from within and drives people to engage in activities that make them happy.

(iii) Which of the following is a mobile operating system?

a. Ubuntu

b. Microsoft Windows

c. Google Android

d. macOS

Answer: c

Reason: Google Android is a mobile operating system designed for smartphones and tablets. Ubuntu, Microsoft Windows, and macOS are operating systems, but they are primarily used for computers, not mobile devices.

(iv) Installing the ________ helps in increasing the performance of the computer.

a. spam files

b. disk cleaner software

c. temporary files

d. extra files

Answer: b

Reason: Disk cleaner software helps remove unnecessary files, such as temporary files and cache, from a computer's hard drive. This can free up space and improve the overall performance of the computer.

(v) Making decisions is an important of ________ an entrepreneur.

a. Misconception

b. hindrance

c. function

d. myth

Answer: c

Reason: Decision-making is a crucial function of an entrepreneur. Entrepreneurs must make important decisions regarding the direction of their business, resource allocation, and strategy to ensure success.

(vi) A/An ________ is a line of work that a person takes for life.

a. Impression

b. commission

c. quality

d. career

Answer: d

Reason: A career is a long-term professional path or occupation that a person pursues throughout their life. It involves the progression of various jobs and roles within a particular field.

2. Answer any 5 out of the given 6 questions. (5X1=5)

(i) State whether the following statement is true or false:

Subsetting helps to focus first on the required set of data.

Answer: True

Reason: Subsetting involves selecting a portion of the data that is relevant to the analysis, making it easier to focus on and analyse the required information without distractions from the entire dataset.

(ii) Which of the following statement is true about median?

a. It is the smallest element of a sorted data set.

b. It is the middle point of a sorted data set.

c. It is the middle point of an unsorted data set.

d. It is the smallest element of an unsorted data set.

Answer: b

Reason: The median is the value that separates a dataset into two equal halves when the data is arranged in ascending or descending order. It represents the middle value of a sorted data set.

(iii) Standard Deviation represents how much the data is spread out around the _______________or an average.

a. Standard deviation

b. Mean deviation

c. Mean

d. Median

Answer: c

Reason: Standard deviation measures the extent to which data points in a dataset deviate from the mean (average) of the dataset. It indicates the amount of variation or dispersion from the mean.

(iv) Two-way relative frequency tables represent the percentage of ________ that fit in each category.

a. Preference

b. data points

c. mean values

d. frequency

Answer: b

Reason: A two-way relative frequency table shows the percentage of data points that fall into each category by dividing the frequency of each category by the total number of data points.

(v) _________ is an example of discrete data.

a. Pass or Fail in a Math Test

b. Length of a road

c. Weather forecast

d. Number of stars

Answer: d

Reason: Discrete data refers to countable, distinct values, such as the number of stars, which can only take whole numbers. Other options like "length of a road" or "weather forecast" represent continuous data.

(vi) Which of the following is not true for discarding the data?

a. This helps us to prevent unauthorized access to the data.

b. It is important for all of us to make sure that we discard the digital data in a proper way.

c. In most of the devices, if you do a soft delete of a particular file, this file deletes from the original space and cannot be restored.

d. With the increased amount and intensity of cyber-attacks, it is important for all of us to make sure that we discard the digital data in a proper way.

Answer: c

Reason: This statement is incorrect because in most devices, a soft delete does not permanently delete the file; instead, it moves the file to a temporary location (like a recycle bin), from which it can be restored. Permanent deletion usually requires a separate action.

3. Answer any 5 out of the given 6 questions. (5X1=5)

(i) Data Merging is the process of combining two or more data sets into a single _______.

a. Data Frame

b. Data Designing

c. Data Graphing

d. Data Handling

Answer: a

Reason: Data merging involves combining multiple datasets into a single data structure, commonly referred to as a "Data Frame" in data analysis, particularly in programming languages like Python and R.

(ii) ______bias is an outcome of seeing what you want to see in the data.

a. Linearity

b. Selection

c. Survivor

d. Confirmation

Answer: d

Reason: Confirmation bias occurs when individuals focus on or interpret data in a way that confirms their pre-existing beliefs or expectations, ignoring evidence that contradicts those beliefs.

(iii) ______is all about counting randomness.

a. Mean

b. Median

c. Probability

d. Graphs

Answer: c

Reason: Probability is the branch of mathematics that deals with the likelihood of events occurring, essentially quantifying and counting randomness.

(iv) ______is an example of real-life implementation of standard deviation.

a. Grading tests

b. Sum of values

c. Sorting of data

d. Spellcheck

Answer: a

Reason: Standard deviation is often used in grading tests to measure the variation in student scores from the average, helping to understand the spread of scores in a class.

(v) The private information that is shared should ______be handled with confidentiality.

a. never

b. sometimes

c. always

d. often

Answer: c

Reason: Private information should always be handled with confidentiality to protect the individual's privacy and prevent unauthorized access or misuse of the data.

(vi) There are two ways in which you can store the data in the __________ format or as a physical copy.

a. analog

b. printed

c. hardcopy

d. digital

Answer: d

Reason: Data can be stored in digital format (electronic storage) or as a physical copy (hardcopy or printed format).

4. Answer any 5 out of the given 6 questions. (5X1=5)

(i) A percentile can be defined as the percentage of the total ordered observations at or __________ it.

a. above

b. equal

c. below

d. not at

Answer: c

Reason: A percentile represents the percentage of data points that fall below a certain value in a dataset. For example, if you are in the 80th percentile, 80% of the data points are below your value.

(ii) The value of a z-score always tells us the number of standard deviations we are away from____________.

a. median

b. mean

c. standard deviation

d. percentile

Answer: b

Reason: A z-score indicates how many standard deviations a data point is from the mean of the dataset. It helps in understanding the position of a data point relative to the mean.

(iii) One-to-one join works by ____________ the data tables using the Primary key.

a. merging

b. deleting

c. inserting

d. concatenating

Answer: a

Reason: In database management, a one-to-one join merges data from two tables using a primary key that uniquely identifies records in both tables, ensuring each record from the first table is linked to one and only one record from the second table.

(iv) Which of the following is true about distribution of an event?

a. It shows no values.

b. It consists of only input values that can be seen.

c. It consists of all possible values but not input values.

d. It consists of both input values that can be seen and also all possible values.

Answer: d

Reason: A distribution in statistics shows all the possible values (both observed and theoretical) of a variable and how frequently each value occurs.

(v) Which of the following is the last step of the Statistical Problem-Solving Process?

a. Analyse the data

b. Formulate statistical investigative questions

c. Interpret the data

d. Collect the data

Answer: c

Reason: The final step in the statistical problem-solving process is to interpret the data after it has been collected and analyzed. This involves drawing conclusions and making decisions based on the analysis.

(vi) Which of the following is used to find out the interquartile range?

a. Values of quartiles

b. Values of percentiles

c. Values of deciles

d. Values of z-score

Answer: a

Reason: The interquartile range (IQR) is calculated using the values of the first quartile (Q1) and the third quartile (Q3) and is the range between these two quartiles (IQR = Q3 - Q1).

5. Answer any 5 out of the given 6 questions. (5X1=5)

(i) The weight of students in a class has a mean of 22 with standard deviation of 4. What is the z-score for a student who weighs 30 kg?

a. 0

b. 1

c. 2

d. 3

Answer: c

Reason: The z-score is calculated using the formula:

z=X−mean/standard deviation.

Here, z=30−22/4=8/4=2.

(ii) The median of the given dataset values 7, 12, 15, 16, 20 is

a. 15

b. 10

c. 11

d. 12

Answer: a

Reason: The median is the middle value of a sorted dataset. Since the data set is already sorted, the median is 15, which is the middle number.

(iii) The mean absolute deviation for the data 3, 5, 9, 10, 15, 16 is

a. 5

b. 3

c. 4

d. 6

Answer: c

Reason: The mean absolute deviation is the average of the absolute differences between each data point and the mean of the dataset. Calculating this gives 4.

(iv) If two coins are tossed at the same time, what is the probability of getting Head-Tail?

a. 0.50

b. 0.45

c. 0.25

d. 0.35

Answer: c

Reason: The possible outcomes when tossing two coins are: HH, HT, TH, TT.

Only one of these (HT or TH) is a Head-Tail combination. The probability is 1/4=0.25.

(v) Data collection designs must acknowledge ____________ in data.

a. Statistical Process Control

b. Test Data

c. Variability

d. Experimental Designs

Answer: c

Reason: Variability in data refers to the degree to which data points in a dataset differ from each other. Effective data collection designs must account for this variability.

(vi) If the data that is fed into the system is ____________model accuracy and fidelity are compromised.

a. biased

b. predictive

c. accurate

d. continuous

Answer: a

Reason: If the data fed into the system is biased, it leads to inaccurate models and compromised fidelity, as the data does not represent the true situation or population accurately.

SECTION B

(Subjective Type Questions) (26 marks)

Answer any 3 out of the given 5 questions on Employability Skills. Answer each question in 20 - 30 words. (3X2=6)

6. What is self-motivation? Give an example.

Answer: Self-motivation is the inner drive to take action and achieve goals without needing pressure or encouragement from others. It's about pushing yourself to do things because you want to, even when it's hard.

Example: Imagine you have a big exam coming up. Instead of waiting for your parents or teachers to remind you to study, you decide to make a study plan and follow it because you want to do well. This is self-motivation—you are taking the initiative to work hard because you care about your success.

7. Explain any two steps for Effective Time Management.

Answer:

1. Make a To-Do List:

Start your day by listing all the tasks you need to do. This helps you stay organized and ensures you don't forget anything important. For example, you might list out your homework, study time, and other activities.

2. Prioritize Your Tasks:

Decide which tasks are the most important and do them first. This way, you make sure the most critical things get done, even if you run out of time for the less important tasks. For instance, if you have a test tomorrow and an assignment due next week, focus on studying for the test first.

8. Define any two of the following:

a. Virus

b. Identity Theft

c. Software Piracy

Answer:

a. Virus: A virus is a type of harmful software that can infect your computer. It spreads from one computer to another and can damage files, slow down your system, or even steal your personal information.

b. Identity Theft: Identity theft happens when someone steals your personal information, like your name, credit card details, or social security number, and uses it without your permission. This can lead to financial loss or damage to your reputation.

c. Software Piracy: Software piracy is the illegal copying, sharing, or using of software without proper permission or a license. This can include downloading paid software for free or using one license on more computers than allowed.

9. What are the two ways of employment in which one can earn a living? Give an example for each.

Answer:

1. Wage Employment: Wage employment is when you work for someone else and get paid a salary or wages. You follow their schedule and do the tasks they assign.

Example: A teacher working at a school earns a monthly salary for teaching students.

2. Self-Employment: Self-employment is when you work for yourself and make money by running your own business or offering services. You are your own boss.

Example: A person running a bakery earns money by selling cakes and bread to customers.

10. What are the qualities of an entrepreneur?

Answer:

1. Creativity: Entrepreneurs are creative and come up with new ideas for businesses or ways to solve problems.

2. Risk-taking: They are willing to take risks, even if they are not sure they will

succeed. They understand that taking chances is part of starting and growing a business.

3. Hardworking: Entrepreneurs work very hard to achieve their goals. They are dedicated and put in a lot of effort to make their business successful.

4. Confidence: They believe in themselves and their ideas. Entrepreneurs are confident that they can achieve their goals and overcome challenges.

5. Decision-making: Entrepreneurs are good at making decisions, often quickly and under pressure. They know that making the right choices is important for the success of their business.

Answer any 4 out of the given 6 questions in 20 - 30 words each. (4X2=8)

11. What is Data-based subsetting? Give an example.

Answer: Data-based subsetting is the process of selecting a specific portion or subset of data from a larger dataset. This allows you to focus on the most relevant information for your analysis without dealing with the entire dataset.

Example: Imagine you have a dataset of 1,000 students' test scores from different schools. If you only want to analyze the scores of students from one particular school, you would create a subset of the data that includes only those students' scores, ignoring the rest. This helps you work with a smaller, more manageable amount of data that's directly related to what you want to study.

12. What is Continuous data? Give an example.

Answer: Continuous data is data that can take any value within a certain range. It can be measured and divided into smaller parts, and it often includes decimals or fractions.

Example: The height of students in a class is an example of continuous data. Heights can be 150.5 cm, 160.2 cm, 165.8 cm, and so on. There are many possible values between any two heights, and you can measure it as precisely as needed.

13. Why is Central Limit Theorem important?

Answer: The Central Limit Theorem (CLT) is important because it helps us understand that when we take a large enough sample from any population, the sample mean (average) will be approximately normally distributed (bell-shaped), even if the original data is not.

Why it's important:

• Predictability: It allows us to make predictions about the population even if we only have a sample.

• Confidence Intervals: It helps in calculating confidence intervals, which tell us how sure we are about our estimates.

• Normal Distribution: Many statistical methods assume normal distribution, and CLT tells us that this assumption is valid when we have large samples.

14. What is Many-to-Many Join? Give an example to support your answer.

Answer: A Many-to-Many Join is a type of database join that occurs when multiple records in one table are related to multiple records in another table. This kind of relationship requires a third table, called a junction or bridge table, to connect the two tables.

Example: Imagine a school database with two tables: one for Students and another for Courses. Each student can enroll in many courses, and each course can have many students. To connect these tables, you create a third table, Enrollments, which records which students are in which courses.

• Students Table: Contains student information like Student ID, Name, etc.

• Courses Table: Contains course information like Course ID, Course Name, etc.

• Enrollments Table: Contains records of Student ID and Course ID, linking students to courses.

15. Name the two ways in which data can be stored. Give an example.

Answer: There are two main ways to store data:

1. Digital Storage:

Data is stored electronically on devices like computers, USB drives, or cloud storage.

Example: Saving a document on your computer's hard drive or uploading photos to Google Drive.

2. Physical Storage:

Data is stored in a physical format, like on paper or printed documents.

Example: A printed report or a book in a library.

These methods ensure that data is preserved and accessible when needed.

16. Define the term percentile. Give an example.

Answer: A percentile is a measure that tells us the value below which a certain percentage of data points fall in a dataset. It helps us understand the relative standing of a particular value within the dataset.

Example: If you score in the 90th percentile on a test, it means that you scored better than 90% of the other students who took the test. If there were 100 students, your score would be higher than 90 of them.

Percentiles are useful for comparing individual scores or values to a larger group.

Answer any 3 out of the given 5 questions in 50 - 80 words each. (3X4=12)

17. Give the steps to calculate Standard Deviation.

Answer: To calculate the Standard Deviation, follow these steps:

1. Find the Mean: Add up all the data points and divide by the number of data points to get the average (mean).
2. Calculate the Differences: Subtract the mean from each data point to find the difference (deviation) for each one.
3. Square the Differences: Square each of the differences to get rid of any negative signs.
4. Find the Mean of Squared Differences: Add up all the squared differences and divide by the number of data points (or by n−1n-1n−1 for a sample) to get the variance.

5. Take the Square Root: Finally, take the square root of the variance to get the Standard Deviation.

18. Explain the following components of the Statistical Problem-Solving Process with example:

a. Formulate statistical investigative questions

b. Collect/Consider the data

Answer:

a. Formulate statistical investigative questions:

• This step involves creating specific questions that you want to answer with your data. These questions guide your entire analysis.

• Example: "What is the average height of students in Class 10?"

b. Collect/Consider the data:

• In this step, you gather the data needed to answer your questions. You must ensure the data is relevant and accurate.

• Example: Measuring the height of each student in Class 10 and recording it in a table.

19. Differentiate between Recall Bias and Survivor Bias. Give an example of each.

Answer: **1. Recall Bias**

Definition: Recall bias occurs when participants or data sources do not remember past events accurately, leading to misreported or incomplete data.

Context: Common in **surveys**, **retrospective studies**, and **self-reported data**.

Example in Data Science: Suppose you're building a model using survey data about past shopping behaviour. If people are asked how many times they purchased groceries last month, they might overestimate or underestimate due to faulty memory. This inaccuracy can lead to misleading patterns in the model.

Key Issue: **Memory distortion** affects the input data.

2. Survivor Bias (Survivorship Bias)

Definition: Survivor bias occurs when only the "survivors" or successful cases are analysed, while ignoring the ones that failed or were excluded, leading to skewed results.

Context: Common in **performance studies**, **product evaluations**, **startup analysis**, etc.

Example in Data Science:

Analysing only successful startups to find the traits of a successful business, without considering the failed ones. If only companies that raised Series B funding are used to train a success-prediction model, the model will miss patterns from startups that failed earlier.

Key Issue: **Missing data** from those who didn't make it through a selection filter.

20. What is the Interquartile Range? Give an example to calculate an interquartile range.

Answer: The Interquartile Range (IQR) is a measure of statistical spread, which tells us the range within which the middle 50% of data points lie. It is calculated by subtracting the first quartile (Q1) from the third quartile (Q3).

Example: Suppose you have the following data set: 2, 4, 6, 8, 10, 12, 14.

1. Find Q1 (first quartile): The median of the lower half (2, 4, 6) is 4.
2. Find Q3 (third quartile): The median of the upper half (10, 12, 14) is 12.
3. Calculate IQR: IQR=Q3−Q1=12−4=8

The Interquartile Range for this data set is 8, meaning the middle 50% of the data lies within this range.

21. Mention any two ways to discard the data stored in physical copy and any two ways to discard digital data.

Answer:

Ways to Discard Physical Data:

1. Shredding: Use a shredder to cut the paper into small pieces, making it unreadable and ensuring that sensitive information cannot be retrieved.
2. Burning: Safely burn the documents to completely destroy the information,

ensuring it cannot be reconstructed or accessed.

Ways to Discard Digital Data:

1. Permanent Deletion (Secure Delete): Use software tools to permanently delete files from your computer, ensuring they cannot be recovered.

2. Disk Formatting: Completely format the storage device (e.g., hard drive, USB) to remove all data, making it difficult to recover.

CBSE Previous Year Solved Question Paper 2024

SUBJECT CODE: 419

SET-4

Q.P. CODE: 106

Instructions:

Please check that this question paper contains **21** questions.

Q.P. Code given on the right-hand side of the question paper should be written on the title page of the answer-book by the candidate.

Please write down the serial number of the question in the answer-book before attempting it.

15-minute time has been allotted to read this question paper. The question paper will be distributed at 10.15 a.m. From 10.15 a.m. to 10.30 a.m., the students will read the question paper only and will not write any answer on the answer-book during this period.

DATA SCIENCE

Time allowed: 2 hours

Maximum Marks: 50

General Instructions:

1. Please read the instructions carefully.
2. This question paper consists of 21 questions in two sections: Section A and Section B.
3. Section A has Objective Type Questions, whereas Section B contains Subjective Type Questions.
4. Out of the given (5 + 16 =) 21 questions, the candidate has to answer (5 + 10 =) 15 questions in the allotted (maximum) time of 2 hours.
5. All questions of a particular section must be attempted in the correct order.
6. Section A: Objective Type Questions (24 marks):
    a. This section has 5 questions.
    b. There is no negative marking.

c. Do as per the instructions given.

d. Marks allotted are mentioned against each question/part.

7. Section B: Subjective Type Questions (26 marks):

a. This section has 16 questions.

b. A candidate has to do 10 questions.

c. Do as per the instructions given.

d. Marks allotted are mentioned against each question/part.

SECTION A

(Objective Type Questions) (24 marks)

1. Answer any 4 out of the given 6 questions on Employability Skills. (4X1=4)

(i) What is a common misconception about starting a business?

a. You need a large amount of money to get started

b. Starting a business requires no financial investment

c. You can start a business with whatever money you have

d. Every business idea has to be unique

Answer: a

Reason: Many people believe that starting a business requires a lot of money, but the reality is that you can start small with the resources you have and grow over time. Some businesses can be started with minimal investment.

(ii) Which of the following is not true with respect to self-awareness abilities?

a. Being self-aware means that you can identify your strengths and weaknesses.

b. Self-awareness helps to convert your strength to weakness.

c. Self-awareness helps to convert your strength to exceptional talent.

d. Analysing your strengths and weaknesses helps you to attain success in life.

Answer: b

Reason: Self-awareness is about recognizing and understanding your strengths and weaknesses, not converting strengths into weaknesses. It helps you use your strengths effectively and work on your weaknesses.

(iii) Managing __________________ is about making a plan to be able to cope effectively with daily pressures and to strike a balance between life, work, relationships, relaxation, and fun.

a. Weight

b. Stress

c. Beliefs

d. Interests

Answer: b

Reason: Managing stress involves planning and balancing various aspects of life to cope effectively with daily pressures, ensuring overall well-being.

(iv) Which of the following is a type of verbal communication?

a. Gestures

b. Body language

c. Facial expressions

d. Interpersonal communication

Answer: d

Reason: Interpersonal communication involves talking and exchanging ideas directly with others, which is a form of verbal communication. Gestures, body language, and facial expressions are non-verbal forms of communication.

(v) What is the keyboard shortcut for copying selected text or files in most operating systems?

a. Ctrl + X

b. Ctrl + Z

c. Ctrl + V

d. Ctrl + C

Answer: d

Reason: The shortcut Ctrl + C is commonly used to copy selected text or files in most operating systems. The other options perform different functions: Ctrl + X cuts, Ctrl + Z undoes, and Ctrl + V pastes.

(vi) How many Sustainable Development Goals (SDGs) were adopted by the United Nations in 2015?

a. 5

b. 10

c. 15

d. 17

Answer: d

Reason: The United Nations adopted 17 Sustainable Development Goals (SDGs) in 2015, aimed at addressing global challenges like poverty, inequality, climate change, and more.

2. Answer any 5 out of the given 6 questions. (5X1=5)

(i) In data analysis, why should you create subsets of your data?

a. To increase the size of your dataset

b. To make the data easier to analyse

c. To add extra information in your dataset

d. To add noise to the data

Answer: b

Reason: Creating subsets of data allows you to focus on the most relevant parts of the data, making analysis more manageable and efficient. This is especially useful when dealing with large datasets.

(ii) Which of the following graphs shows the probability distribution for tossing a coin?

a. 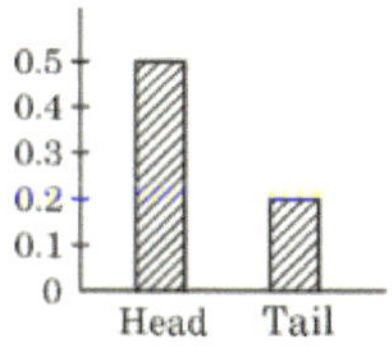

b. 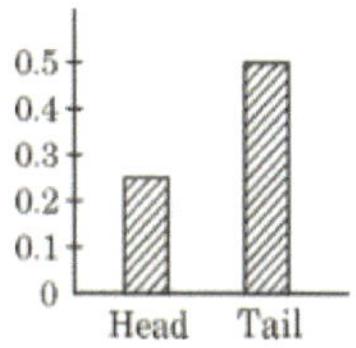

c. 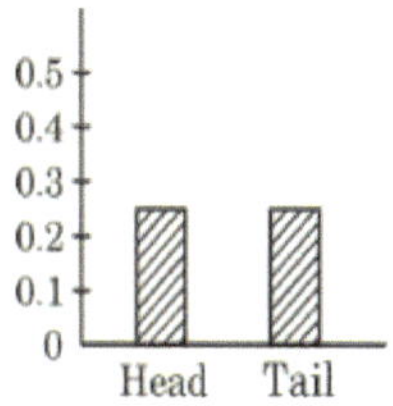

d. 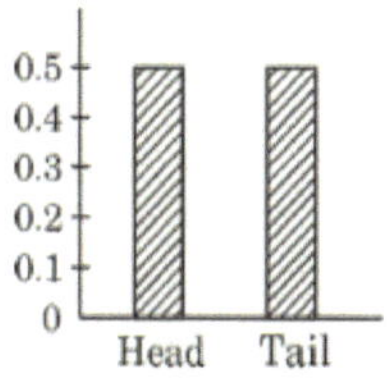

Answer: d

Reason: When tossing a fair coin, the probability of getting a Head or a Tail is equal, which is 0.5 for each. Graph d correctly shows this equal probability distribution for both Head and Tail, with both bars reaching the 0.5 mark.

(iii) In Data Science, _____________ is a deviation from the expected outcome in the data.

a. Outlier

b. Standard Deviation

c. Bias

d. Variance

Answer: a

Reason: An outlier is a data point that significantly differs from other observations in a dataset. It represents a deviation from the expected outcome, often indicating an anomaly or an error in data collection or entry.

(iv) Identify the type of join from the following diagram.

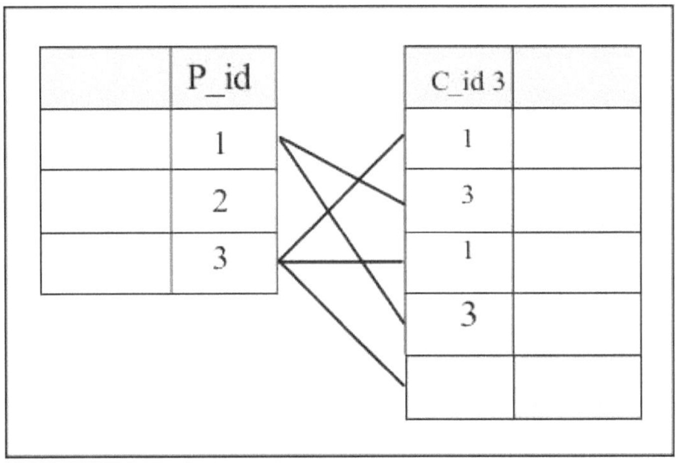

a. Many to Many

b. One to Many

c. One to One

d. Many to One

Answer: a

Reason:

The diagram shows that each p_id can be linked to multiple c_id values, and each c_id can be linked to multiple p_id values. This is a classic example of a Many to Many relationships, where entries in both tables can be associated with multiple entries in the other table.

(v) State True or False.

If you soft delete a particular file, it gets deleted permanently and cannot be restored.

Answer: False

Reason: Soft deleting a file usually means the file is moved to a "Recycle Bin" or

"Trash," from where it can be restored. It is not permanently deleted.

(vi) Statement I: Shredding and cutting are two ways to discard physical data. Statement II: The shredded documents can be read easily but the documents that are cut down into small pieces cannot be read.

a. Both statement I and Statement II are true

b. Both statement I and Statement II are false

c. Statement I is true, but Statement II is false

d. Statement II is true, but Statement I is false

Answer: c

Reason: Shredding documents into small pieces is a secure method to prevent the data from being read or reconstructed, while cutting might not be as secure.

3. Answer any 5 out of the given 6 questions. (5X1=5)

(i) A _____________ table represents the percentage of data points that fit in each category.

a. Dummy

b. Two-way frequency

c. Two-way relative frequency

d. Two-way direct frequency

Answer: c

Reason: A two-way relative frequency table shows the percentage of data points that fit within each category of two variables.

(ii) The value of z-score is always ___________ if the value of z-score lies above the mean.

a. Positive

b. Negative

c. Zero

d. Infinite

Answer: a

Reason: A z-score above the mean is positive because the data point is greater than the average.

(iii) What does a distribution represent in Data Science?

a. The exact values for a variable and how often they occur

b. The probable values for a variable and how often they occur

c. The average values for a variable and how often they occur

d. The maximum values for a variable and how often they occur

Answer: b

Reason: A distribution in data science often represents the probable values for a variable and the frequency with which they occur.

(iv) In which bias do we assume that change in one quantity produces an equal and proportional change in another?

a. Linearity Bias

b. Confirmation Bias

c. Recall Bias

d. Selection Bias

Answer: a

Reason: Linearity bias occurs when we assume a linear relationship (proportional change) between two variables, even when it may not exist.

(v) Which of the following is an appropriate way of discarding physical copies of confidential data?

a. Crumbing the papers which contain confidential data and throwing them in the dustbin

b. Burning the documents

c. Leaving the confidential data in an unlocked drawer

d. Using the papers containing confidential data for rough work.

Answer: b

Reason: Burning is a secure method to ensure that physical copies of confidential data cannot be recovered.

(vi) Quartiles of a dataset partition the data in _________ equal parts.

a. Three

b. Four

c. Six

d. Eight

Answer: b

Reason: Quartiles divide a dataset into four equal parts, each representing 25% of the data.

4. Answer any 5 out of the given 6 questions. (5X1=5)

(i) What security measure should you employ to ensure that even in the case of a data leak, the hackers are not able to read your data ?

a. Backing up data to an external drive

b. Using any password

c. Encrypting the data

d. Deleting the data

Answer: c

Reason: Encryption makes the data unreadable to unauthorized users, even if it is leaked.

(ii) In a dataset of income levels for a small town's residents, the income data includes a few extremely high values (outliers) due to the presence of some wealthy individuals. In the scenario, which form of central tendency would be more appropriate to describe the typical income of the town's residents?

a. Mean

b. Median

c. Mode

d. Range

Answer: b

Reason: The median is less affected by outliers and provides a better measure of central tendency in this case.

(iii) What is the correct order of steps in the Statistical Problem Solving Process?

a. Collect/Consider the data, formulate statistical investigative questions, Analyse the data, Interpret the results

b. Analyse the data, Interpret the results, Collect/Consider the data, Formulate statistical investigative questions

c. Formulate statistical investigative questions, Collect/Consider the data, Interpret the results, Analyse the data

d. Formulate statistical investigative questions, Collect/Consider the data, Analyse the data, Interpret the results

Answer: d

Reason: This is the logical sequence for solving a statistical problem.

(iv) If n is the total number of data in a sample, which of the following correctly represents the first decile?

a. D1 = 1 * (n+1) / 10th Data

b. D1 = 1 + (n+1) / 10th Data

c. D1 = 1 (n+1) / 10th Data

d. D1 = 1 / (n+1) / 10th Data

Answer: a

Reason: The first decile (D1) is calculated as 1/10th of the sorted data.

(v) If you have a dataset with 100 data points, what data point defines the first quartile (Q1)?

a. The 25th percentile

b. The 50th percentile

c. The 75th percentile

d. The 100th percentile

Answer: a

Reason: The first quartile (Q1) corresponds to the 25th percentile of the data.

(vi) Which type of bias is commonly associated with recommendation systems, polls, and personalised advertisements, where the sample data is not representative of the true future population of cases that the model will see?

a. Linearity Bias

b. Recall Bias

c. Selection Bias

d. Survivor Bias

Answer: c

Reason: Selection bias occurs when the data used to train a model does not represent the true population, leading to skewed results.

5. Answer any 5 out of the given 6 questions. (5X1=5)

(i) Statement I: In Data Science, we can perform data merging by implementing data joins on the databases in frame.

Statement II: There are five categories of data joins.

a. Both statement I and statement II are correct

b. Both statement I and statement II are incorrect

c. Statement I is correct, but statement II is incorrect

d. Statement I is incorrect, but statement II is correct

Answer: Reason: Statement I is correct about data merging, but there are generally four main types of joins (Inner, Left, Right, and Full joins).

(ii) You have a dataset of ages for a group of 5 people. The ages are as follows: 25, 32, 29, 35 and 27. What is the median age for this dataset?

a. 27

b. 28

c. 29

d. 30

Answer: c

Reason: The median is the middle value when the numbers are arranged in order (25, 27, 29, 32, 35).

(iii) You have a bag with two red marbles and two green marbles. If you randomly select one marble from the bag without looking, what is the probability that it will be a red marble?

a. 0·50

b. 0·25

c. 1·0

d. 0·75

Answer: a

Reason: There are 2 red marbles out of 4 total marbles, so the probability is 0.50 or 50%.

(iv) In statistical analysis, what minimum sample size is generally considered enough for the Central Limit Theorem to hold?

a. 5

b. 10

c. 20

d. 30

Answer: d

Reason: A sample size of 30 is often considered the minimum for the Central Limit Theorem to apply.

(v) Deciles sort the data into how many equal parts?

a. 5

b. 10

c. 9

d. 8

Answer: b

Reason: Deciles divide a dataset into 10 equal parts, each containing 10% of the data points.

(vi) Assertion (A): Privacy does not always mean confidentiality of data.

Reason (R): Private data may need to be audited based on the relevant requirements.

a. Both (A) and (R) are correct and (R) is the correct explanation of (A).

b. Both (A) and (R) are correct, but (R) is not the correct explanation of (A).

c. (A) is correct, but (R) is incorrect.

d. (R) is correct, but (A) is incorrect.

Answer: a

Reason: Privacy and confidentiality are related but not the same. Private data may require audits under certain conditions, which can be a correct and necessary process.

SECTION B

(Subjective Type Questions) (26 marks)

Answer any 3 out of the given 5 questions on Employability Skills. Answer each question in 20 30 words. (3X2=6)

6. Give any two ways to overcome barriers of effective communication.

Answer:

1. Listen Actively: Pay full attention to the speaker without interrupting. This helps you understand the message clearly and reduces misunderstandings.
2. Ask Questions: If something is unclear, ask questions to clarify. This ensures that both parties are on the same page and improves overall communication.

7. Differentiate between wage employed people and self-employed people.

Answer:

1. Wage-Employed People:

• Work for an employer and receive a fixed salary or wages.

• Follow a schedule and tasks set by the employer.

• Example: A teacher working in a school.

2. Self-Employed People:

• Work for themselves and generate their own income.

• Set their own schedule and manage their own business.

• Example: A person running their own bakery.

8. Explain any two key strategies or initiatives that can contribute towards achieving Sustainable Development Goals (SDGs).

Answer:

1. Promoting Renewable Energy: Using renewable energy sources like solar, wind, and hydro power helps reduce reliance on fossil fuels, lowering carbon emissions and contributing to climate action (SDG 13).

2. Reducing Plastic Waste: Cutting down on single-use plastics and encouraging recycling helps protect oceans and wildlife, supporting life below water (SDG 14) and sustainable cities (SDG 11).

These strategies help create a healthier environment and promote sustainability for future generations.

9. Define any two of the following terms:

a. ICT

b. Trojan horse

c. Firewall

Answer:

a. ICT (Information and Communication Technology):

ICT refers to technologies that provide access to information and help people communicate. This includes tools like computers, the internet, and mobile phones that allow us to connect, share, and process information.

b. Trojan Horse:

A Trojan horse is a type of malicious software that pretends to be a useful or harmless program. Once installed, it can damage your computer or steal your personal information without you knowing.

c. Firewall:

A firewall is a security system that protects your computer or network from unauthorized access. It acts like a barrier, controlling what data can enter or leave your system, keeping out hackers and harmful software.

10. What does the acronym SMART stand for in the context of goal setting? Why is goal setting an essential factor in your personal life?

Answer:

SMART stands for:

- Specific: Clearly define what you want to achieve.
- Measurable: Make sure you can track your progress.
- Achievable: Set a goal that is realistic and attainable.
- Relevant: Ensure the goal is important to you and aligns with your values.
- Time-bound: Set a deadline for when you want to achieve the goal.

Why Goal Setting is Important: Goal setting helps you focus on what you want to achieve in life. It gives you direction, motivation, and a clear path to follow. By setting SMART goals, you can break down big dreams into smaller, manageable steps, making it easier to accomplish them.

Answer any 4 out of the given 6 questions in 20 - 30 words each. (4X2=8)

11. Discuss any two ways of protecting confidential data that is stored in digital form.

Answer:

1. Encryption: Encrypt data to make it unreadable to unauthorized users, ensuring

only those with the decryption key can access it.

2. Strong Passwords: Use strong, unique passwords and enable two-factor authentication to protect access to digital data from unauthorized users.

12. Write steps to calculate Mean Absolute Deviation (MAD).

Answer:

- Find the Mean: Calculate the average of all data points.
- Calculate Deviations: Subtract the mean from each data point and take the absolute value.
- Find MAD: Average the absolute deviations to get the Mean Absolute Deviation (MAD).

13. Explain the concept of Recall Bias in Statistics.

Answer: Recall Bias occurs when people forget or inaccurately remember past events, leading to incorrect or skewed data. This is common in surveys or studies where participants are asked to recall past experiences, resulting in data that may not be entirely reliable.

14. For each of the following scenarios, classify the data as either discrete or continuous:

a. Result of an admission test

b. Weight of apples at a grocery store

c. Football score in a match

d. Depth of a river

Answer:

a. Result of an admission test - Discrete

b. Weight of apples at a grocery store - Continuous

c. Football score in a match - Discrete

d. Depth of a river – Continuous

15. Explain one-to-one join with the help of an example.

Answer: A one-to-one join is when you combine two tables in a database, where each record in the first table matches exactly one record in the second table.

Example: Imagine you have two tables:

- Table 1: Employees (Employee ID, Name)
- Table 2: Employee Addresses (Employee ID, Address)

If each employee has only one address, you can join these tables using the Employee ID as the key. The result will be a combined table where each employee's name is matched with their address.

This type of join ensures that every row in one table has a corresponding row in the other table.

16. In a dataset representing the ages of a group of people, the lower quartile (Q1) is 30 years, and the upper quartile (Q3) is 50 years. Calculate the interquartile range (IQR) for this dataset.

Answer:

To calculate the Interquartile Range (IQR):

IQR=Q3−Q1

Given:

- Q1=30
- Q3=50

IQR=50−30=20 years

So, the Interquartile Range (IQR) is 20 years. This means that the middle 50% of ages in the dataset fall within a 20-year range.

Answer any 3 out of the given 5 questions in 50 - 80 words each. (3X4=12)

17. What is a two-way frequency table? Explain its features with a suitable example.

Answer: A two-way frequency table is a table that shows the frequency (number of occurrences) of data points across two different categories. It helps in analysing the relationship between two variables by displaying how often each combination of categories occurs.

Features:

• Rows and Columns: The table has rows and columns representing the two different categories.

• Frequency Count: Each cell in the table shows the frequency of data points that fall into both the corresponding row and column categories.

• Totals: The table often includes row and column totals, which show the sum of frequencies for each category.

Example: Imagine a survey of 50 students on their preference for morning or evening study sessions and their grade level (9th or 10th grade). The table could look like this:

	9th Grade	10th Grade	Total
Morning	15	10	25
Evening	5	20	25
Total	20	30	50

18. Explain the following components of the Statistical Problem Solving Process:

a. Analyse the data

b. Interpret the results

Answer: a. Analyse the data:

• This step involves examining the collected data to find patterns, trends, or relationships. It includes calculating statistics like mean, median, and standard deviation, or creating graphs and charts to visualize the data. The goal is to make sense of the raw data and prepare it for drawing conclusions.

b. Interpret the results:

• After analysing the data, this step involves understanding what the results mean in the context of the original problem or question. It's about explaining the findings, making inferences, and deciding what the data tells us. For example, if the analysis shows that students who study in the morning perform better, the interpretation would focus on why this might be the case and how it can be applied in real situations.

19. Explain Central Limit Theorem. Give any two real world scenarios in which it is used.

Answer: The Central Limit Theorem (CLT) states that if you take many samples from a population and calculate their averages, the distribution of those averages will form a normal (bell-shaped) distribution, even if the original data isn't normally distributed. This is true as long as the sample size is large enough.

Real-world scenarios where CLT is used:

1. Quality Control in Manufacturing: Factories use CLT to ensure that the average quality of products is consistent. By sampling a few products from each batch, they can predict the overall quality of all products.
2. Polling and Surveys: Pollsters use CLT to predict election outcomes. They survey a small group of people and use the sample averages to estimate the opinions of the entire population.

The CLT helps in making reliable predictions and decisions based on sample data.

20. What is z-score in data science? Write the formula to calculate z-score. Also explain the importance of z-score in data science.

Answer: A z-score in data science is a measure that tells us how far a data point is from the mean of a dataset, in terms of standard deviations. It shows whether the data point is above or below the mean.

Formula: z-score=X−μ/σ

Where:

- X = value of the data point
- μ= mean of the dataset
- σ = standard deviation of the dataset

Importance of z-score:

- Standardization: Z-scores allow us to compare data points from different distributions by standardizing them.
- Outlier Detection: Z-scores help identify outliers, which are data points that are

significantly different from others in the dataset.

- Probability Calculation: Z-scores are used in calculating probabilities in a normal distribution, making them essential for statistical analysis.

Z-scores are crucial in data analysis for understanding the relative position of data points and making meaningful comparisons.

21. You are a data analyst working for a healthcare organisation. Your team is responsible for analysing patient data to improve healthcare services and outcomes. Ethical considerations are crucial in handling this sensitive information. Recently, you received a dataset containing patient records, including medical history, personal information, and treatment details.

(i) What is the most important ethical consideration when handling patient's data?

a. Data accuracy and quality

b. Data sharing with external organisations without patients knowledge

c. Data storage cost optimisation

d. Patient's privacy protection

Answer: d. Patient's privacy protection

Explanation:

The most important ethical consideration when handling patient data is patient privacy protection. This means ensuring that sensitive personal and medical information is kept confidential and is only accessed or shared with proper authorization. Protecting patient privacy is crucial to maintaining trust and complying with legal and ethical standards in healthcare.

(ii) A colleague suggests using patient's data to train an artificial intelligence model without the patients consent. What is your ethical stance on this suggestion?

a. Support the idea as it can lead to technological advancements

b. Implement the idea without informing the patients

c. Reject the idea and ensure patient consent is obtained for any data usage

d. Share the colleague's idea with other organisations for wider adoption

Answer: c. Reject the idea and ensure patient consent is obtained for any data usage

Explanation:

Using patient data without their consent is unethical and violates their privacy rights. It's important to reject the idea and ensure that patients are fully informed and provide their consent before their data is used, especially for purposes like training AI models. This approach respects patient autonomy and complies with ethical standards in data usage.

(iii) List any two ethical guidelines around data analysis.

Answer:

1. Data Privacy and Confidentiality: Always ensure that personal and sensitive data is kept private and secure. Data should only be accessed by authorized individuals and used for the intended purpose. This protects individuals' rights and maintains trust.

2. Informed Consent: Before collecting or using data, obtain clear consent from the individuals involved. They should be fully informed about how their data will be used, stored, and shared. This ensures transparency and respects individuals' autonomy over their personal information.

CBSE Previous Year Question Paper 2025

SUBJECT CODE: 419

SET-4

Q.P. CODE: 106

Instructions:

Please check that this question paper contains **21** questions.

Q.P. Code given on the right-hand side of the question paper should be written on the title page of the answer-book by the candidate.

Please write down the serial number of the question in the answer-book before attempting it.

15-minute time has been allotted to read this question paper. The question paper will be distributed at 10.15 a.m. From 10.15 a.m. to 10.30 a.m., the students will read the question paper only and will not write any answer on the answer-book during this period.

DATA SCIENCE

Time allowed: 2 hours

Maximum Marks: 50

General Instructions:

1. Please read the instructions carefully.
2. This question paper consists of 21 questions in two sections: Section A and Section B.
3. Section A has Objective Type Questions, whereas Section B contains Subjective Type Questions.
4. Out of the given (5 + 16 =) 21 questions, the candidate has to answer (5 + 10 =) 15 questions in the allotted (maximum) time of 2 hours.
5. All questions of a particular section must be attempted in the correct order.
6. Section A: Objective Type Questions (24 marks):

a. This section has 5 questions.

b. There is no negative marking.

c. Do as per the instructions given.

d. Marks allotted are mentioned against each question/part.

7. Section B: Subjective Type Questions (26 marks):

a. This section has 16 questions.

b. A candidate has to do 10 questions.

c. Do as per the instructions given.

d. Marks allotted are mentioned against each question/part.

SECTION A

(Objective Type Questions) (24 Marks)

1. Answer any *4* out of the given *6* questions on Employability Skills. (4X1=4)

(i) Which of the following is *not* true for communication?

(A) The receiver transmits the message through one medium or another.

(B) The receiver listens or understands the message.

(C) The receiver conveys his/her understanding of the message to the sender in the form of feedback to complete the communication cycle.

(D) The word 'communication' comes from the Latin word commūnicāre, meaning 'to share'.

Correct Answer: (A) The receiver transmits the message through one medium or another.

Reason:
In communication, **the sender** is the one who **transmits the message** through a medium (e.g., speech, writing).
The **receiver receives and interprets** the message.
Therefore, **(A) is false** — it's not the receiver who transmits the message.

(ii) Having the ability to work independently means ___________.

(A) not accepting mistakes

(B) stop learning after a certain point

(C) becoming self-aware, self-monitoring and self-correcting

(D) blaming others for the slightest mistake

Correct Answer: (C) becoming self-aware, self-monitoring and self-correcting

Reason:
Working independently means you can manage your own work without constant supervision.
This involves:

- Being **self-aware** (understanding your strengths and weaknesses)
- **Self-monitoring** your progress
- **Self-correcting** when mistakes occur
  These are essential traits of an independent worker.

(iii) __________ is our ability to do the things that need to be done without someone or something influencing us.

(A) Self-management (B) Self-motivation

(C) Self-control (D) Self-care

Correct Answer: (B) Self-motivation

Reason:
Self-motivation is the internal drive to take action without external pressure.
It reflects doing things because you *want* to and not because someone else is telling you.
Options like self-management and self-control are related but not as directly tied to *internal drive*.

(iv) __________ are computer programs that can damage the data and software programs or steal the information stored on a computer.

(A) Viruses (B) Theft

(C) Antivirus (D) BIOS

Correct Answer: (A) Viruses

Reason:
Viruses are malicious software designed to damage or disrupt computer systems, steal data, or corrupt files.
They are harmful programs — unlike antivirus software, which is protective.

(v) __________ is the type of self-employment where one is running a business to satisfy the needs of people and looking for ways to make the business better to make profits.

(A) Wage employment

(B) Services

(C) Creativity

(D) Entrepreneurship

Correct Answer: (D) Entrepreneurship

Reason:
Entrepreneurship involves:

- Starting and running a business
- Solving problems or fulfilling needs
- Seeking innovation and growth
- Earning profits
  It is a type of self-employment focused on value creation and risk-taking.

(vi) __________ is the development that satisfies the needs of the present without compromising the capacity of future generations, guaranteeing the balance between economic growth, care for the environment and social well-being.

(A) Sustainable development

(B) Economic development

(C) Personal development

(D) Global development

Correct Answer: (A) Sustainable development

Reason:
Sustainable development emphasizes:

- Meeting current needs
- Protecting future generations' ability to meet theirs
- Balancing **economic**, **environmental**, and **social** goals
  It's a globally recognized principle (e.g., by the UN) for long-term development.

2. Answer any *5* out of the given *6* questions. *(5 X 1=5)*

(i) The median is the middle point of a/an __________ data set.

(A) Unsorted

(B) Sorted

(C) Grouped

(D) Labelled

Correct Answer: (B) Sorted

Reason:
To find the **median**, the data must be **arranged in order** (sorted), either ascending or descending.
You **cannot** correctly identify the middle value from an **unsorted** list.

(ii) What does a distribution represent in Data Science?

(A) A method which shows the probable values for a variable and how often they occur.

(B) It is the measure of how spread out the numbers are.

(C) It is the average of how far away all values in a data set are from the mean.

(D) The maximum values for a variable and how often they occur.

Correct Answer: (A) A method which shows the probable values for a variable and how often they occur.

Reason:
In data science, a **distribution** tells us:

- What values a variable can take
- How frequently those values occur
  Examples: Normal distribution, uniform distribution, etc.

(iii) Confirmation Bias is also known as ___________.

(A) Recall Bias

(B) Selection Bias

(C) Observer Bias

(D) Linearity Bias

Correct Answer: (C) Observer Bias

Reason:
Confirmation bias (also called **observer bias**) is the tendency to:

- Look for or interpret data in a way that confirms one's pre-existing beliefs.
  This often leads to ignoring contradicting evidence.

(iv) In Data Science, ___________ is the process of combining two or more data sets into a single data frame.

(A) Pattern

(B) Data merging

(C) Distribution

(D) Probability

Correct Answer: (B) Data merging

Reason:
Data merging refers to:

- Combining datasets using common columns or keys
  It is often used when data is spread across multiple sources (e.g., merging customer info with transaction history).

(v) ___________ does not always mean confidentiality because private data may need to be audited based on the relevant requirements.

(A) Privacy

(B) Data governance

(C) Ethical guidelines

(D) Bias

Correct Answer: (A) Privacy

Reason:
Privacy is about **individual control** over personal information.
However, privacy doesn't always imply **full confidentiality**, especially in cases like audits, legal compliance, or security checks.

(vi) State True or False :

The private data acquired from a person with their consent should be exposed for use by different businesses or individuals.

Correct Answer: False

Reason:
Even if data is collected with **consent**, it should **only** be used for the **specific purpose** for which consent was given.
Sharing it with other parties **without additional consent** is unethical and often illegal (e.g., GDPR violations).

3. Answer any *5* out of the given *6* questions. *(5 X 1=5)*

(i) While interpreting two-way tables, categories are placed in ________ column and ________ row.

(A) bottom, right

(B) top, left

(C) top, right

(D) bottom, left

Correct Answer: (B) top, left

Reason:
In a **two-way table**, the **column headings (top)** and **row labels (left)** define the categories being compared.

(ii) The statistical problem-solving process involves mainly ________ component(s).

(A) One

(B) Two

(C) Three

(D) Four

Correct Answer: (D) Four

Reason:
The four steps are:

1. Formulate a statistical question

2. Collect data

3. Analyze data

4. Interpret results

(iii) Assertion (A) : Biased models tend to discriminate against certain groups of people.

Reason (R) : It is very important to eliminate the bias to avoid these risks.

(A) Both Assertion (A) and Reason (R) are true and Reason (R) is the correct explanation of Assertion (A).

(B) Both Assertion (A) and Reason (R) are true, but Reason (R) is *not* the correct explanation of Assertion (A).

(C) Assertion (A) is true, but Reason (R) is false.

(D) Assertion (A) is false, but Reason (R) is true.

Correct Answer: (A) Both Assertion (A) and Reason (R) are true and Reason (R) is the correct explanation of Assertion (A).

Reason:
Biased models can lead to unfair decisions. Eliminating bias is essential to ensure fairness and ethical AI use.

(iv) ___________ is also known as standard score as it allows comparison of scores on different types of variables by standardizing the distribution.

(A) Joins

(B) Z-Score

(C) Percentiles

(D) Distribution

Correct Answer: (B) Z-Score

Reason:
A **Z-Score** indicates how many standard deviations a value is from the mean, allowing comparisons across distributions.

(v) The one-to-one join works by merging the data tables using the __________ key.

(A) Basic

(B) Secondary

(C) Primary

(D) Alternate

Correct Answer: (C) Primary

Reason:
A **primary key** uniquely identifies each record in a table and is used to match records during joins.

(vi) The private information that is shared should always be handled ____________.

(A) Irresponsibly

(B) with Confidentiality

(C) Emotionally

(D) Carelessly

Correct Answer: (B) with Confidentiality

Reason:
Private data must be protected and handled with confidentiality to ensure trust and legal compliance.

4. Answer any *5* out of the given *6* questions. *(5X1=5)*

(i) In Data Science, what is a subset?

Answer:

A **subset** is a **smaller selection** of rows or columns taken from a larger dataset. Example: Filtering customers from a specific city in a larger customer data table.

(ii) Distribution in statistics is defined by underlying ___________ and not by the graph.

(A) Probabilities

(B) Median

(C) Mean

(D) Analysis

Correct Answer: (A) Probabilities

Reason:
The **shape of the distribution** comes from **how probabilities** are distributed across values, not from the graph itself.

(iii) The __________ states that the distribution of sample mean nears normal distribution as the sample size gets bigger.

(A) Probability

(B) Central Limit Theorem

(C) Identifying Patterns

(D) Distribution

Correct Answer: (B) Central Limit Theorem

Reason:
The **Central Limit Theorem (CLT)** says the sampling distribution of the mean approaches normality as sample size increases.

(iv) The Z-Score is always __________ if the value of Z-Score lies above the mean and it is __________ if its value is below the mean.

(A) Positive, Negative

(B) Negative, Positive

(C) Positive, Zero

(D) Negative, Zero

Correct Answer: (A) Positive, Negative

Reason:
Z-scores:

- **Positive**: value is **above the mean**
- **Negative**: value is **below the mean**

(v) A/An __________ can be defined as the measure of the middle 50% of the values when ordered from lowest to highest.

(A) Percentile

(B) Quartile

(C) Interquartile range

(D) Z-Score

Correct Answer: (C) Interquartile range

Reason:
The **interquartile range (IQR)** = Q3 - Q1, which measures the spread of the **middle 50%** of data.

(vi) Data should institutionalize unfair means. (True/False)

Correct Answer: False

Reason:
Data practices should promote **fairness**, **transparency**, and **ethical use**, not unfairness.

5. Answer any *5* out of given *6* questions. (*5X1=5)*

(i) Mean is a measure of central tendency. (True/False)

Correct Answer: True

Reason:
Mean is one of the main ways to find the **center** of a data set (along with median and mode).

(ii) Depth of an ocean, weight of a person or length of a road are examples of __________ data.

(A) Discrete

(B) Qualitative

(C) Fixed

(D) Continuous

Correct Answer: (D) Continuous

Reason:
These are **measurable quantities** that can take **any value within a range**, making them **continuous** data.

(iii) We can use ____________ to predict how likely or unlikely particular events may be.

(A) Distribution

(B) Probability

(C) Partiality

(D) Random Experiment

Correct Answer: (B) Probability

Reason:
Probability is used to **quantify likelihood** of outcomes in uncertain situations.

(iv) The mathematical formula for calculating the Z-Score is Z = (x – y)/y, where x = raw score, X = mean.

What does X stand for ?

(A) Standard Deviation

(B) Median

(C) Distribution

(D) Percentile

Correct Answer: (C) Distribution

(v) A __________ can be defined as the percentage of the total ordered observations at or below it.

(A) Standard Deviation

(B) Percentile

(C) Mean

(D) Median

Correct Answer: (B) Percentile

Reason:
A **percentile** shows the percentage of data values **at or below** a certain point in the distribution.

(vi) Once we are done with the user data, especially confidential data, it is important that we ___________ this data.

(A) Sell

(B) Misuse

(C) Discard

(D) Forward

Correct Answer: (C) Discard

Reason:
Confidential data should be **safely discarded or anonymized** to protect privacy and avoid misuse.

SECTION B

(Subjective Type Questions) (26 Marks)

Answer any 3 out of the given 5 questions based on Employability Skills in 20 – 30 words each. (3X2=6)

6. What is Interpersonal Communication? Give an example to explain it.

Answer: Interpersonal communication is the exchange of ideas or feelings between two or more people.

Example: Talking to your friend about homework.

7. List any four stress management techniques.

Answer:

1. Deep breathing
2. Exercise
3. Listening to music
4. Talking to someone you trust

8. What is the purpose of an antivirus software?

Answer: Antivirus software protects the computer from harmful programs like viruses that can damage files or steal data.

9. "A person needs a lot of money to start a business."

Answer: Is this statement a fact or myth ? Justify your answer.

It is a **myth**. Many businesses can start with small money, like online selling or home-based work.

10. Briefly discuss any two major problems related to Sustainable Development.

Answer:

Pollution: It harms the environment and health.

Overuse of resources: It leaves less for future generations.

Answer any 4 out of the given 6 questions in 20 – 30 words each. (4X2=8)

11. What is Standard Deviation? Give an example

Answer: Standard Deviation shows how much the data values vary from the average. **Example**: In test scores, a low standard deviation means most students scored similarly.

12. Briefly explain the term Discrete Data with the help of an example.

Answer: Discrete data includes countable values.

Example: Number of books on a shelf (you can count them as 1, 2, 3, etc.).

13. What is Recall Bias? Why does it occur?

Answer: Recall bias happens when people forget past events incorrectly while giving information. It occurs mainly in surveys or interviews where memory is needed.

14. Why is the Z-score so important? Give any two key points.

Answer:

Z-score shows how far a value is from the average.

It helps compare different data sets with different units.

15. What is One-to-many Join? Give an example to support your answer.

Answer: One-to-many join connects one record from a table to many records in another.

Example: One teacher teaches many students.

16. While safely discarding the physical copies of confidential data, mention any one situation in which cutting the documents into pieces is considered an appropriate method. Also mention any one point to consider while cutting the documents into pieces to ensure the successful discarding of the data.

Answer: Situation: Cutting documents with personal details like bank info is appropriate.

Point to consider: Cut papers into very small pieces so no one can reassemble them.

Answer any 3 out of the given 5 questions in 50 – 80 words each. (3X4=12)

17. List down the steps to find standard deviation.

Answer:

- **Find the mean** of the data set.
- **Subtract the mean** from each value and square the result.
- **Add** all the squared values.
- **Divide** the total by the number of values (for population) or by (n-1) for sample.
- **Take the square root** of the result.

This final value is the **standard deviation**, which shows data spread.

18. What is Uniform distribution? Make a probability table for tossing two coins.

Answer: Uniform distribution means **each outcome has an equal chance** of happening.
When tossing two coins, each result is equally likely.
Sample space: HH, HT, TH, TT

Probability Table:

Outcome	Probability
HH	1/4
HT	1/4
TH	1/4
TT	1/4

Each outcome has a **0.25 (25%) chance**.

19. With reference to Data Science, answer the following questions:

(a) What is Bias?

(b) Why does it occur?

(c) Why is it important to eliminate the Bias? Discuss in detail.

Answer:

(a) What is Bias?
Bias is an error in data or model that gives unfair or incorrect results.

(b) Why does it occur?
It happens due to wrong data, poor sampling, or personal opinions in data collection.

(c) Why is it important to eliminate the Bias?
Bias must be removed to ensure **fair, accurate, and ethical results**, especially in fields like hiring, healthcare, and education, where it can hurt certain groups.

20. List down the steps to calculate decile.

Answer:

- **Arrange data** in ascending order.

- **Find position** using formula: $D_k = (k/10) \times (n + 1)$, where *k* is the decile number and *n* is total values.

- **Locate the value** at the calculated position.

- If needed, use interpolation to get exact decile value.

Deciles divide data into 10 equal parts, helpful in comparing performance or income levels.

21. Explain the need and ways to discard digital data.

Answer:

Discarding digital data is important to protect **privacy and prevent misuse** of personal or confidential information.
Ways to discard data include:

Deleting and emptying recycle bin

Using data-wiping software

Resetting devices to factory settings

Physically destroying storage media like hard drives

This ensures the data cannot be recovered or used by others later.

Unit Wise Solved Sample Papers on Board Papers

CBSE Board Pattern Question Paper

Class X – Data Science (844)

Unit 1: Data Governance

Time: 1 Hour

Maximum Marks: 25

Section A: Objective Type Questions (1 × 5 = 5 Marks)

Q1. Data governance mainly deals with:

a) Data storage only

b) Data privacy and management

c) Data deletion

d) Data printing

Answer: b) Data privacy and management

Q2. Which of the following refers to protecting personal data?

a) Data Mining

b) Data Privacy

c) Data Cleaning

d) Data Sorting

Answer: b) Data Privacy

Q3. Unauthorized access to data is called:

a) Data Integrity

b) Data Breach

c) Data Mining

d) Data Analysis

Answer: b) Data Breach

Q4. GDPR is related to:

a) Data Visualization

b) Data Security Law

c) Data Collection

d) Data Storage

Answer: b) Data Security Law

Q5. Data ethics refers to:

a) Legal storage of data

b) Moral use of data

c) Data analysis

d) Data backup

Answer: b) Moral use of data

Section B: Short Answer Questions (2 × 5 = 10 Marks)

Q6. Define Data Governance.

Answer:

Data governance refers to the overall management of data availability, usability, integrity, and security in an organization. It ensures that data is handled properly, remains accurate, and is protected from misuse. It includes policies, standards, and procedures that guide how data is collected, stored, and used. Effective data governance helps organizations maintain trust, comply with legal requirements, and make better decisions using reliable data.

Q7. What is Data Privacy?

Answer:

Data privacy is the process of protecting personal and sensitive information from unauthorized access or misuse. It ensures that individuals have control over how their data is collected, stored, and shared. Data privacy includes practices like encryption, secure storage, and user consent. It is important for maintaining trust and complying with laws such as GDPR.

Q8. Explain Data Ethics with an example.

Answer:

Data ethics involves the responsible and fair use of data. It ensures that data is not used in a way that harms individuals or violates their rights. For example, a company should not sell customer data without permission. Ethical use of data builds trust and prevents misuse, discrimination, or bias in decision-making systems.

Q9. What is Data Ownership?

Answer:

Data ownership refers to the rights and responsibilities of individuals or organizations over data. The owner has control over how data is used, shared, and protected. For example, a user owns their personal information on social media platforms and has the right to control its usage.

Q10. What is Data Security?

Answer:

Data security involves protecting data from unauthorized access, corruption, or theft. It includes techniques like encryption, firewalls, and access control. Strong data security ensures confidentiality, integrity, and availability of data, which are essential for safe data handling.

Section C: Long Answer Questions (5 × 2 = 10 Marks)

Q11. Explain the importance of Data Governance in an organization.

Answer:

Data governance is important because it ensures that data is accurate, secure, and used responsibly. It helps organizations maintain data quality, which is essential for making correct decisions. It also protects sensitive information from cyber threats and unauthorized access. Proper governance ensures compliance with laws and regulations, avoiding legal penalties. Additionally, it improves efficiency by standardizing data processes and enhancing trust among stakeholders. Without proper data governance, organizations may face data loss, security breaches, and poor decision-making.

Q12. Discuss Data Privacy and Data Security. How are they different?

Answer:

Data privacy and data security are closely related but different concepts. Data privacy focuses on protecting personal information and ensuring it is used appropriately with consent. It deals with policies and rights of individuals. On the other hand, data security focuses on protecting data from unauthorized access using technical measures like encryption and firewalls. While privacy is about “who can use data,” security is about "how data is protected." Both are important for safeguarding information and maintaining trust.

Unit 2: Exploratory Data Analysis (EDA)

With complete answers (exam-ready format)

QUESTION PAPER

Time: 1.5 Hours

Maximum Marks: 30

Section A: Objective Type Questions (1 × 10 = 10 Marks)

Q1. EDA stands for:

a) External Data Access

b) Exploratory Data Analysis

c) Efficient Data Algorithm

d) Embedded Data Analysis

Answer: b

Q2. Which step comes first in EDA?

a) Visualization

b) Data Cleaning

c) Data Collection

d) Data Modeling

Answer: c

Q3. Removing duplicate data is part of:

a) Data Collection

b) Data Cleaning

c) Data Visualization

d) Data Storage

Answer: b

Q4. Which tool is commonly used for visualization?

a) Notepad

b) Excel

c) Paint

d) Calculator

Answer: b

Q5. Pie charts are used to show:

a) Trends

b) Proportions

c) Relationships

d) Predictions

Answer: b

Q6. Which graph is best for trends over time?

a) Bar chart

b) Line chart

c) Pie chart

d) Histogram

Answer: b

Q7. Mean is a measure of:

a) Position

b) Central tendency

c) Spread

d) Shape

Answer: b

Q8. Outliers are:

a) Average values

b) Extreme values

c) Missing values

d) Duplicate values

Answer: b

Q9. Scatter plot shows:

a) Distribution

b) Relationship between variables

c) Proportions

d) Categories

Answer: b

Q10. Histogram is used for:

a) Continuous data distribution

b) Text data

c) Images

d) Tables

Answer: a

Section B: Short Answer Questions (2 × 5 = 10 Marks)

Q11. Define Exploratory Data Analysis (EDA).

Answer:

Exploratory Data Analysis (EDA) is the process of analyzing datasets to summarize their main characteristics using statistical techniques and visualization tools. It helps in understanding data patterns, detecting anomalies, and preparing data for further analysis or modeling.

Q12. What is Data Cleaning?

Answer:

Data cleaning is the process of removing errors, inconsistencies, missing values, and duplicate records from a dataset. It ensures that the data is accurate, reliable, and ready for analysis.

Q13. What is Data Visualization?

Answer:

Data visualization is the graphical representation of data using charts, graphs, and plots. It helps in understanding complex data easily and identifying patterns and trends.

Q14. What is an Outlier?

Answer:

An outlier is a data point that is significantly different from other values in a dataset. It may occur due to errors or unusual observations and can affect analysis results.

Q15. Define Mean and Median.

Answer:

Mean is the average of all values in a dataset, calculated by dividing the sum of values by the number of values. Median is the middle value when the data is arranged in ascending or descending order.

Section C: Long Answer Questions (5 × 2 = 10 Marks)

Q16. Explain the steps involved in Exploratory Data Analysis.

Answer:

EDA involves several steps. First, data is collected from various sources. Then, data cleaning is performed to remove errors and missing values. After that, data transformation may be done to organize it properly. Visualization techniques such as graphs and charts are used to explore patterns. Finally, statistical methods are applied to summarize the data and draw conclusions. These steps help in better understanding and decision-making.

Q17. Explain different types of data visualization techniques.

Answer:

Data visualization techniques include bar charts, pie charts, line graphs, histograms, and scatter plots. Bar charts are used for comparison, pie charts show proportions, line graphs display trends over time, histograms show distribution of continuous data, and scatter plots reveal relationships between variables. These techniques make data easier to interpret and analyze.

Section D: Case Study (2 × 5 = 10 Marks)

Case:

A school collects marks of students. Some entries are missing, and teachers want to analyze performance trends using charts.

Q18. What issue is present in the dataset?

Answer: Missing values

Q19. Which process should be applied first?

Answer: Data cleaning

Q20. Which chart is best to compare student marks?

Answer: Bar chart

Q21. Which graph is best to show performance trend over time?

Answer: Line graph

Q22. Why is visualization important here?

Answer:

Visualization helps teachers easily understand student performance, identify trends, and make better academic decisions.

Unit 3: Classification Algorithms (Decision Tree & KNN)

Includes complete answers (exam-ready format)

QUESTION PAPER

Time: 1.5 Hours

Maximum Marks: 30

Section A: Objective Type Questions (1 × 10 = 10 Marks)

Q1. Classification is used to:

a) Predict continuous values

b) Group similar data

c) Assign categories

d) Clean data

Answer: c

Q2. Which is a classification algorithm?

a) Linear Regression

b) Decision Tree

c) Clustering

d) Histogram

Answer: b

Q3. Decision Tree consists of:

a) Tables

b) Nodes and branches

c) Rows and columns

d) Graphs

Answer: b

Q4. The top node in a Decision Tree is called:

a) Leaf node

b) Root node

c) Branch node

d) End node

Answer: b

Q5. KNN stands for:

a) Known Node Network

b) K-Nearest Neighbors

c) Kernel Node Network

d) Key Network Node

Answer: b

Q6. KNN works based on:

a) Distance

b) Time

c) Speed

d) Size

Answer: a

Q7. Which value of K is commonly used?

a) 0

b) 1

c) Negative values

d) Fractions

Answer: b

Q8. Classification output is:

a) Numerical value

b) Category or label

c) Graph

d) Table

Answer: b

Q9. Accuracy measures:

a) Speed

b) Correct predictions

c) Data size

d) Data type

Answer: b

Q10. Leaf nodes represent:

a) Input data

b) Final decision/output

c) Graph

d) Model

Answer: b

Section B: Short Answer Questions (2 × 5 = 10 Marks)

Q11. Define Classification.

Answer:

Classification is a machine learning technique used to assign data into predefined categories or classes. It is commonly used in applications like spam detection and disease prediction.

Q12. What is a Decision Tree?

Answer:

A Decision Tree is a supervised learning algorithm used for classification. It splits data into branches based on conditions and provides a final decision at leaf nodes.

Q13. What is KNN Algorithm?

Answer:

K-Nearest Neighbors (KNN) is a classification algorithm that classifies a data point based on the majority class of its nearest neighbors.

Q14. What is Accuracy?

Answer:

Accuracy is the measure of how many predictions made by a model are correct out of total predictions.

Q15. What is a Root Node?

Answer:

The root node is the topmost node in a decision tree from which all decisions and branches begin.

Section C: Long Answer Questions ($5 \times 2 = 10$ Marks)

Q16. Explain how Decision Tree works.

Answer:

A Decision Tree works by splitting data into smaller subsets based on conditions. It starts from the root node and divides data using decision rules. Each branch represents a choice, and leaf nodes represent final outcomes. It continues splitting until the data is classified properly. It is easy to understand and widely used in decision-making problems.

Q17. Explain KNN algorithm with an example.

Answer:

KNN works by finding the nearest data points to a new data point based on distance. For example, if K = 3, the algorithm looks at the 3 nearest neighbors and assigns the majority class. If most neighbors belong to class A, the new data point is classified as A. It is simple but can be slow for large datasets.

Section D: Case Study ($2 \times 5 = 10$ Marks)

Case:

A bank wants to classify whether a loan applicant is "Approved" or "Rejected" based on income and credit score.

Q18. Which technique should be used?

Answer: Classification

Q19. Which algorithm can be used here?

Answer: Decision Tree / KNN

Q20. What type of output will the model give?

Answer: Category (Approved/Rejected)

Q21. Which factor helps KNN classify applicants?

Answer: Distance from nearest neighbors

Q22. What metric can be used to evaluate the model?

Answer: Accuracy

Unit 4: Regression Algorithms (Linear & Multiple Regression)

Includes complete answers (exam-ready format)

QUESTION PAPER

Time: 1.5 Hours

Maximum Marks: 30

Section A: Objective Type Questions ($1 \times 10 = 10$ Marks)

Q1. Regression is used to:

a) Classify data

b) Predict continuous values

c) Group data

d) Clean data

Answer: b

Q2. Linear regression shows relationship between:

a) One dependent and one independent variable

b) Two dependent variables

c) Categories only

d) Images

Answer: a

Q3. The output of regression is:

a) Category

b) Label

c) Numerical value

d) Graph

Answer: c

Q4. Which is a regression algorithm?

a) Decision Tree

b) KNN

c) Linear Regression

d) Clustering

Answer: c

Q5. The equation of linear regression is:

a) $x + y = z$

b) $y = mx + c$

c) $x^2 + y^2$

d) y/x

Answer: b

Q6. In $y = mx + c$, m represents:

a) Intercept

b) Slope

c) Error

d) Data

Answer: b

Q7. In $y = mx + c$, c represents:

a) Slope

b) Intercept

c) Error

d) Variable

Answer: b

Q8. Multiple regression involves:

a) One input variable

b) Multiple input variables

c) No variables

d) Only output

Answer: b

Q9. Regression is useful for:

a) Sorting

b) Forecasting

c) Cleaning

d) Clustering

Answer: b

Q10. Best fit line minimizes:

a) Distance errors

b) Time

c) Size

d) Speed

Answer: a

Section B: Short Answer Questions ($2 \times 5 = 10$ Marks)

Q11. Define Regression.

Answer:

Regression is a machine learning technique used to predict continuous numerical values based on relationships between variables. It helps in forecasting and trend analysis.

Q12. What is Linear Regression?

Answer:

Linear regression is a method that models the relationship between a dependent variable and an independent variable using a straight line equation.

Q13. What is Multiple Regression?

Answer:

Multiple regression is an extension of linear regression where multiple independent variables are used to predict a single dependent variable.

Q14. What is Slope?

Answer:

Slope represents the rate of change of the dependent variable with respect to the independent variable. It shows how steep the line is.

Q15. What is Intercept?

Answer:

Intercept is the value of the dependent variable when the independent variable is zero. It is represented by ‘c’ in the equation.

Section C: Long Answer Questions ($5 \times 2 = 10$ Marks)

Q16. Explain Linear Regression with an example.

Answer:

Linear regression establishes a relationship between two variables using a straight line. The equation above represents this relationship, where y is the dependent variable, x is the independent variable, m is the slope, and c is the intercept.

For example, if we want to predict a student's marks based on hours studied, linear regression can help. If hours increase, marks are expected to increase proportionally. The model finds the best-fit line that minimizes errors between predicted and actual values.

Q17. Explain Multiple Regression and its applications.

Answer:

Multiple regression uses more than one independent variable to predict a dependent variable. For example, house price prediction may depend on size, location, and number of rooms. It improves prediction accuracy by considering multiple factors. It is widely used in finance, healthcare, and business forecasting.

Section D: Case Study (2 × 5 = 10 Marks)

Case:

A company wants to predict sales based on advertisement spending and product price.

Q18. Which technique should be used?

Answer: Regression

Q19. Which type of regression is suitable here?

Answer: Multiple Regression

Q20. What will be the output?

Answer: Continuous value (Sales prediction)

Q21. What does slope indicate in this case?

Answer:

It shows how much sales change with respect to advertisement spending or price.

Q22. Why is regression useful here?

Answer:

Regression helps predict future sales and supports better business decisions.

Unit 5: Unsupervised Learning (Clustering)

Includes complete answers (exam-ready format)

QUESTION PAPER

Time: 1.5 Hours

Maximum Marks: 30

Section A: Objective Type Questions ($1 \times 10 = 10$ Marks)

Q1. Unsupervised learning is used when:

a) Data is labeled

b) Data is unlabeled

c) Data is deleted

d) Data is sorted

Answer: b

Q2. Clustering is a type of:

a) Supervised learning

b) Unsupervised learning

c) Regression

d) Classification

Answer: b

Q3. Clustering groups data based on:

a) Random selection

b) Similarity

c) Size

d) Speed

Answer: b

Q4. Which is a clustering algorithm?

a) KNN

b) Decision Tree

c) K-Means

d) Linear Regression

Answer: c

Q5. Number of clusters in K-Means is represented by:

a) X

b) Y

c) K

d) Z

Answer: c

Q6. Unsupervised learning does NOT require:

a) Data

b) Labels

c) Patterns

d) Analysis

Answer: b

Q7. Clustering is useful for:

a) Prediction

b) Grouping data

c) Cleaning data

d) Sorting data

Answer: b

Q8. Customer segmentation is an example of:

a) Regression

b) Classification

c) Clustering

d) Visualization

Answer: c

Q9. K-Means algorithm works by:

a) Finding nearest categories

b) Assigning labels

c) Grouping based on centroids

d) Sorting data

Answer: c

Q10. Outliers in clustering are:

a) Normal points

b) Extreme values

c) Categories

d) Labels

Answer: b

Section B: Short Answer Questions (2 × 5 = 10 Marks)

Q11. Define Unsupervised Learning.

Answer:

Unsupervised learning is a type of machine learning where the model works on unlabeled data to identify patterns and relationships. It does not require predefined outputs and is mainly used for clustering and grouping data.

Q12. What is Clustering?

Answer:

Clustering is a technique used to group similar data points together based on their characteristics. It helps in identifying hidden patterns in data.

Q13. What is K-Means Algorithm?

Answer:

K-Means is a clustering algorithm that divides data into K groups by assigning data points to the nearest cluster center (centroid) and updating the centroids iteratively.

Q14. What is a Centroid?

Answer:

A centroid is the center point of a cluster. It represents the average position of all data points in that cluster.

Q15. What are Outliers?

Answer:

Outliers are data points that are significantly different from other data points. They can affect clustering results.

Section C: Long Answer Questions (5 × 2 = 10 Marks)

Q16. Explain how K-Means clustering works.

Answer:

K-Means clustering works by dividing data into K clusters. First, K centroids are selected randomly. Then, each data point is assigned to the nearest centroid based on distance. After that, centroids are recalculated as the mean of assigned points. This process repeats until centroids stabilize. It helps in grouping similar data efficiently.

Q17. Explain applications of clustering.

Answer:

Clustering is used in many fields such as customer segmentation, image processing, market research, and recommendation systems. For example, companies group customers based on buying behavior to target marketing strategies. It helps in discovering hidden patterns in large datasets.

Section D: Case Study (2 × 5 = 10 Marks)

Case:

An e-commerce company wants to group customers based on purchasing behavior to improve marketing strategies.

Q18. Which technique should be used?

Answer: Clustering

Q19. Which type of learning is this?

Answer: Unsupervised Learning

Q20. Which algorithm can be used?

Answer: K-Means

Q21. What is the benefit of grouping customers?

Answer:

It helps in targeted marketing and better customer understanding.

Q22. What determines similarity between customers?

Answer:

Features such as purchase history, spending habits, and preferences.

Unit 6: Data Governance (Advanced / Revision Level)

Includes complete answers (exam-ready format)

QUESTION PAPER

Time: 1.5 Hours

Maximum Marks: 30

Section A: Objective Type Questions ($1 \times 10 = 10$ Marks)

Q1. Data governance ensures:

a) Data duplication

b) Data quality and security

c) Data deletion

d) Data printing

Answer: b

Q2. Data privacy focuses on:

a) Data storage

b) Protecting personal information

c) Data cleaning

d) Data analysis

Answer: b

Q3. Unauthorized access to data is called:

a) Data mining

b) Data breach

c) Data sorting

d) Data entry

Answer: b

Q4. Data ethics deals with:

a) Speed of data

b) Moral use of data

c) Size of data

d) Format of data

Answer: b

Q5. GDPR is related to:

a) Data visualization

b) Data protection law

c) Data cleaning

d) Data grouping

Answer: b

Q6. Data ownership means:

a) Deleting data

b) Controlling data usage

c) Sharing data

d) Printing data

Answer: b

Q7. Data security includes:

a) Charts

b) Encryption

c) Graphs

d) Tables

Answer: b

Q8. Which is a threat to data?

a) Encryption

b) Backup

c) Hacking

d) Storage

Answer: c

Q9. Confidentiality means:

a) Data sharing

b) Data protection from unauthorized access

c) Data cleaning

d) Data grouping

Answer: b

Q10. Integrity in data means:

a) Data duplication

b) Data accuracy

c) Data deletion

d) Data storage

Answer: b

Section B: Short Answer Questions (2 × 5 = 10 Marks)

Q11. Define Data Governance.

Answer:

Data governance is the process of managing data availability, usability, security, and integrity within an organization. It ensures proper handling of data through policies and standards.

Q12. What is Data Privacy?

Answer:

Data privacy refers to protecting personal and sensitive information from unauthorized access and ensuring it is used with consent.

Q13. What is Data Security?

Answer:

Data security involves protecting data from threats such as hacking, unauthorized access, and data breaches using techniques like encryption and firewalls.

Q14. What is Data Ethics?

Answer:

Data ethics refers to the responsible and fair use of data without harming individuals or violating their rights.

Q15. What is Data Breach?

Answer:

A data breach is an incident where sensitive data is accessed or disclosed without authorization.

Section C: Long Answer Questions ($5 \times 2 = 10$ Marks)

Q16. Explain the importance of Data Governance.

Answer:

Data governance is important because it ensures data accuracy, security, and compliance with legal regulations. It helps organizations make better decisions using reliable data. It also protects sensitive information from cyber threats and builds trust among users. Without proper governance, organizations may face data loss, misuse, and legal issues.

Q17. Differentiate between Data Privacy and Data Security.

Answer:

Data privacy focuses on protecting personal data and ensuring it is used with consent. Data security focuses on protecting data from unauthorized access using technical measures like encryption. Privacy is about “who can use data,” while security is about “how data is protected.” Both are essential for safe data management.

Section D: Case Study (2 × 5 = 10 Marks)

Case:

A company collects customer information but fails to secure it properly. Hackers access the data, and customers complain about misuse.

Q18. What issue occurred in the company?

Answer: Data breach

Q19. Which concept was violated?

Answer: Data privacy

Q20. What should the company implement to prevent this?

Answer: Data security measures (encryption, firewalls)

Q21. Which law helps protect user data?

Answer: GDPR

Q22. What should company take from customers before using data?

Answer: User consent

Unit 7: Exploratory Data Analysis (Advanced / Revision Level)

Includes complete answers (exam-ready format)

QUESTION PAPER

Time: 1.5 Hours

Maximum Marks: 30

Section A: Objective Type Questions ($1 \times 10 = 10$ Marks)

Q1. Exploratory Data Analysis is used to:

a) Store data

b) Analyze and summarize data

c) Delete data

d) Print data

Answer: b

Q2. Which step is performed first in EDA?

a) Visualization

b) Data cleaning

c) Data collection

d) Modeling

Answer: c

Q3. Removing missing values is part of:

a) Data visualization

b) Data cleaning

c) Data grouping

d) Data storage

Answer: b

Q4. Which chart is best for showing proportions?

a) Line chart

b) Bar chart

c) Pie chart

d) Scatter plot

Answer: c

Q5. Which graph shows trends over time?

a) Pie chart

b) Line graph

c) Histogram

d) Table

Answer: b

Q6. Mean is a measure of:

a) Dispersion

b) Central tendency

c) Shape

d) Range

Answer: b

Q7. Median is:

a) Highest value

b) Lowest value

c) Middle value

d) Average of squares

Answer: c

Q8. Histogram is used for:

a) Categorical data

b) Continuous data distribution

c) Text data

d) Image data

Answer: b

Q9. Outliers are:

a) Normal values

b) Extreme values

c) Missing values

d) Duplicate values

Answer: b

Q10. Scatter plot shows:

a) Categories

b) Relationship between variables

c) Proportions

d) Tables

Answer: b

Section B: Short Answer Questions (2 × 5 = 10 Marks)

Q11. Define Exploratory Data Analysis (EDA).

Answer:

EDA is the process of analyzing datasets using statistical methods and visualization tools to understand patterns, detect anomalies, and summarize data.

Q12. What is Data Cleaning?

Answer:

Data cleaning is the process of removing errors, missing values, and duplicates from data to improve its quality.

Q13. What is Data Visualization?

Answer:

Data visualization is the graphical representation of data using charts and graphs to make it easier to understand.

Q14. What is an Outlier?

Answer:

An outlier is a data point that is significantly different from other values in the dataset.

Q15. What is the difference between Mean and Median?

Answer:

Mean is the average of all values, while median is the middle value in an ordered dataset. Median is less affected by outliers compared to mean.

Section C: Long Answer Questions (5 × 2 = 10 Marks)

Q16. Explain the steps involved in EDA.

Answer:

EDA involves data collection, data cleaning, data transformation, data visualization, and statistical analysis. First, data is collected from sources. Then errors and missing values are removed. Data is organized and visualized using graphs. Finally, statistical methods are used to identify patterns and insights for decision-making.

Q17. Explain different types of graphs used in EDA.

Answer:

Common graphs include bar charts, pie charts, line graphs, histograms, and scatter plots. Bar charts compare categories, pie charts show proportions, line graphs display trends over time, histograms show distribution of continuous data, and scatter plots show relationships between variables.

Section D: Case Study ($2 \times 5 = 10$ Marks)

Case:

A company analyzes sales data. The dataset contains missing values and outliers. The company wants to understand sales trends and relationships.

Q18. What issue is present in the dataset?

Answer: Missing values and outliers

Q19. Which step should be performed first?

Answer: Data cleaning

Q20. Which graph is best to show sales trend?

Answer: Line graph

Q21. Which graph is used to show relationship between variables?

Answer: Scatter plot

Q22. Why is EDA important in this case?

Answer:

EDA helps identify patterns, trends, and errors in data, enabling better decision-making.

Unit 8: Classification Algorithms – II (KNN & Model Evaluation)

Includes complete answers (exam-ready format)

QUESTION PAPER

Time: 1.5 Hours

Maximum Marks: 30

Section A: Objective Type Questions ($1 \times 10 = 10$ Marks)

Q1. KNN stands for:

a) Known Node Network

b) K-Nearest Neighbors

c) Kernel Neural Network

d) Key Network Node

Answer: b

Q2. KNN is used for:

a) Regression only

b) Classification

c) Sorting

d) Cleaning

Answer: b

Q3. KNN works based on:

a) Time

b) Distance

c) Speed

d) Size

Answer: b

Q4. Value of K represents:

a) Number of variables

b) Number of neighbors

c) Number of outputs

d) Number of datasets

Answer: b

Q5. Small value of K may lead to:

a) Overfitting

b) Underfitting

c) No error

d) No output

Answer: a

Q6. Large value of K may lead to:

a) Overfitting

b) Underfitting

c) High accuracy

d) No change

Answer: b

Q7. Accuracy measures:

a) Data size

b) Correct predictions

c) Data speed

d) Data format

Answer: b

Q8. Which metric is used for evaluation?

a) Accuracy

b) Speed

c) Size

d) Shape

Answer: a

Q9. KNN is a:

a) Supervised learning algorithm

b) Unsupervised algorithm

c) Regression only algorithm

d) Visualization tool

Answer: a

Q10. Distance in KNN is usually calculated using:

a) Mean

b) Median

c) Euclidean distance

d) Mode

Answer: c

Section B: Short Answer Questions (2 × 5 = 10 Marks)

Q11. Define KNN algorithm.

Answer:

K-Nearest Neighbors (KNN) is a supervised learning algorithm used for classification. It classifies a data point based on the majority class of its nearest neighbors.

Q12. What is the role of K in KNN?

Answer:

K represents the number of nearest neighbors considered for classification. It affects the model's accuracy and performance.

Q13. What is Accuracy?

Answer:

Accuracy is the ratio of correct predictions to total predictions made by a model.

Q14. What is Overfitting?

Answer:

Overfitting occurs when a model performs well on training data but poorly on new data because it learns noise instead of patterns.

Q15. What is Underfitting?

Answer:

Underfitting occurs when a model is too simple and fails to capture patterns in the data, leading to poor performance.

Section C: Long Answer Questions (5 × 2 = 10 Marks)

Q16. Explain how KNN algorithm works.

Answer:

KNN works by calculating the distance between a new data point and existing data points. It selects the K nearest neighbors based on distance. Then it assigns the class that is most common among these neighbors. The algorithm is simple but can be computationally expensive for large datasets.

Q17. Explain model evaluation in classification.

Answer:

Model evaluation measures how well a model performs. Accuracy is the most common metric, which shows the percentage of correct predictions. Other metrics include precision and recall. Evaluation helps improve model performance and ensures reliability.

Section D: Case Study (2 × 5 = 10 Marks)

Case:

A hospital uses KNN to classify whether a patient has a disease based on symptoms and medical history.

Q18. Which algorithm is used here?

Answer: KNN

Q19. What type of learning is this?

Answer: Supervised learning

Q20. What does K represent?

Answer: Number of nearest neighbors

Q21. What happens if K = 1?

Answer:

Model may overfit and be sensitive to noise.

Q22. Why is accuracy important here?

Answer:

Accuracy ensures correct disease prediction, which is critical for patient treatment.

Unit 9: Classification Algorithms – II (Model Training, Testing & Evaluation)

Includes complete answers (exam-ready format)

QUESTION PAPER

Time: 1.5 Hours

Maximum Marks: 30

Section A: Objective Type Questions (1 × 10 = 10 Marks)

Q1. Model training means:

a) Cleaning data

b) Teaching model using data

c) Deleting data

d) Sorting data

Answer: b

Q2. Testing data is used to:

a) Train model

b) Evaluate model

c) Clean data

d) Store data

Answer: b

Q3. Accuracy is defined as:

a) Incorrect predictions

b) Correct predictions / total predictions

c) Data size

d) Data type

Answer: b

Q4. Overfitting occurs when:

a) Model is too simple

b) Model memorizes training data

c) Model fails to learn

d) Model is deleted

Answer: b

Q5. Underfitting occurs when:

a) Model is too complex

b) Model is too simple

c) Model is accurate

d) Model is perfect

Answer: b

Q6. Which dataset is used for evaluation?

a) Training data

b) Testing data

c) Raw data

d) Cleaned data

Answer: b

Q7. Precision measures:

a) Total predictions

b) Correct positive predictions

c) Incorrect predictions

d) Data size

Answer: b

Q8. Recall measures:

a) Total predictions

b) Correct detection of actual positives

c) Data type

d) Data speed

Answer: b

Q9. Confusion matrix is used for:

a) Cleaning data

b) Evaluating classification model

c) Sorting data

d) Visualization

Answer: b

Q10. Model evaluation helps to:

a) Delete data

b) Improve model performance

c) Store data

d) Print data

Answer: b

Section B: Short Answer Questions ($2 \times 5 = 10$ Marks)

Q11. What is Model Training?

Answer:

Model training is the process of teaching a machine learning model using training data so that it can learn patterns and relationships.

Q12. What is Model Testing?

Answer:

Model testing is the process of evaluating a trained model using unseen data to check its performance and accuracy.

Q13. Define Accuracy.

Answer:

Accuracy is the ratio of correct predictions made by the model to the total number of predictions.

Q14. What is Overfitting?

Answer:

Overfitting occurs when a model learns training data too well, including noise, and performs poorly on new data.

Q15. What is Underfitting?

Answer:

Underfitting occurs when a model is too simple and fails to capture important patterns in data.

Section C: Long Answer Questions ($5 \times 2 = 10$ Marks)

Q16. Explain the difference between Training and Testing.

Answer:

Training involves feeding data to a model so it can learn patterns. Testing involves evaluating the trained model on new, unseen data to check its performance. Training helps build the model, while testing ensures its reliability and accuracy.

Q17. Explain evaluation metrics in classification.

Answer:

Evaluation metrics include accuracy, precision, recall, and confusion matrix. Accuracy measures overall correctness, precision measures correct positive predictions, recall measures how well actual positives are identified, and confusion matrix shows detailed prediction results. These metrics help assess model performance.

Section D: Case Study ($2 \times 5 = 10$ Marks)

Case:

A company builds a model to classify emails as spam or not spam. The model performs very well on training data but poorly on new emails.

Q18. What problem is seen here?

Answer: Overfitting

Q19. Which dataset is giving good performance?

Answer: Training data

Q20. Which dataset shows poor performance?

Answer: Testing data

Q21. How can this problem be reduced?

Answer:

By using more data, simplifying the model, or applying regularization.

Q22. Why is model evaluation important here?

Answer:

It ensures the model performs well on real-world data and is reliable.

Unit 10: Regression Algorithms – I (Linear Regression & Prediction)

Includes complete answers (exam-ready format)

QUESTION PAPER

Time: 1.5 Hours

Maximum Marks: 30

Section A: Objective Type Questions ($1 \times 10 = 10$ Marks)

Q1. Regression is used to:

a) Classify data

b) Predict continuous values

c) Group data

d) Clean data

Answer: b

Q2. Linear regression models relationship between:

a) Categories

b) Two variables

c) Images

d) Tables

Answer: b

Q3. The output of regression is:

a) Label

b) Category

c) Numerical value

d) Graph

Answer: c

Q4. Which is a regression equation?

a) $x + y$

b) $y = mx + c$

c) $x^2 + y^2$

d) x/y

Answer: b

Q5. In the equation, m represents:

a) Intercept

b) Slope

c) Error

d) Output

Answer: b

Q6. In the equation, c represents:

a) Slope

b) Intercept

c) Error

d) Variable

Answer: b

Q7. Best fit line minimizes:

a) Data size

b) Errors

c) Time

d) Speed

Answer: b

Q8. Regression is useful for:

a) Sorting

b) Forecasting

c) Cleaning

d) Clustering

Answer: b

Q9. Linear regression assumes:

a) No relationship

b) Linear relationship

c) Random relation

d) No data

Answer: b

Q10. Which graph is used in regression?

a) Pie chart

b) Scatter plot

c) Bar chart

d) Histogram

Answer: b

Section B: Short Answer Questions (2 × 5 = 10 Marks)

Q11. Define Regression.

Answer:

Regression is a technique used to predict continuous numerical values based on relationships between variables.

Q12. What is Linear Regression?

Answer:

Linear regression is a method that models the relationship between two variables using a straight line.

Q13. What is Slope?

Answer:

Slope represents the rate of change of the dependent variable with respect to the independent variable.

Q14. What is Intercept?

Answer:

Intercept is the value of the dependent variable when the independent variable is zero.

Q15. What is Prediction in regression?

Answer:

Prediction is the process of estimating future values using a regression model.

Section C: Long Answer Questions (5 × 2 = 10 Marks)

Q16. Explain Linear Regression with equation.

Answer:

Linear regression is used to model the relationship between a dependent variable and an independent variable. The equation shown represents a straight line, where y is the predicted value, x is the input variable, m is the slope, and c is the intercept.

For example, if we predict marks based on study hours, the model finds the best-fit line that minimizes error and gives accurate predictions.

Q17. Explain applications of regression.

Answer:

Regression is widely used in predicting sales, weather forecasting, stock market trends, and demand forecasting. It helps businesses and organizations make informed decisions based on data trends.

Section D: Case Study (2 × 5 = 10 Marks)

Case:

A company wants to predict sales based on advertisement spending.

Q18. Which technique should be used?

Answer: Regression

Q19. What type of regression is used?

Answer: Linear Regression

Q20. What will be the output?

Answer: Continuous value (sales prediction)

Q21. What does slope indicate here?

Answer:

It shows how sales change with advertisement spending.

Q22. Why is regression useful in this case?

Answer:

It helps predict future sales and supports better business planning.

Unit 11: Regression Algorithms – II (Multiple Regression & Model Evaluation)

Includes complete answers (exam-ready format)

QUESTION PAPER

Time: 1.5 Hours

Maximum Marks: 30

Section A: Objective Type Questions ($1 \times 10 = 10$ Marks)

Q1. Multiple regression is used when:

a) One input variable

b) Multiple input variables

c) No variables

d) Only output

Answer: b

Q2. Multiple regression predicts:

a) Categories

b) Continuous values

c) Clusters

d) Labels

Answer: b

Q3. Which is an example of multiple regression?

a) Predicting marks from hours only

b) Predicting marks from hours and attendance

c) Sorting data

d) Clustering data

Answer: b

Q4. Multiple regression equation includes:

a) One variable

b) Multiple variables

c) No variables

d) Only constants

Answer: b

Q5. Regression models are evaluated using:

a) Accuracy only

b) Error measures

c) Speed

d) Size

Answer: b

Q6. Which term represents prediction error?

a) Residual

b) Mean

c) Median

d) Mode

Answer: a

Q7. Best model has:

a) Maximum error

b) Minimum error

c) No data

d) Maximum size

Answer: b

Q8. Regression evaluation checks:

a) Data size

b) Model performance

c) Data type

d) Data speed

Answer: b

Q9. Multiple regression improves:

a) Data cleaning

b) Prediction accuracy

c) Data storage

d) Data deletion

Answer: b

Q10. Forecasting uses:

a) Classification

b) Regression

c) Clustering

d) Sorting

Answer: b

Section B: Short Answer Questions ($2 \times 5 = 10$ Marks)

Q11. Define Multiple Regression.

Answer:

Multiple regression is a technique used to predict a dependent variable using two or more independent variables.

Q12. What is a Residual?

Answer:

Residual is the difference between the actual value and the predicted value in a regression model.

Q13. What is Model Evaluation?

Answer:

Model evaluation is the process of assessing how well a model performs using error measures and performance metrics.

Q14. Why is multiple regression useful?

Answer:

It improves prediction accuracy by considering multiple factors affecting the outcome.

Q15. What is Prediction Error?

Answer:

Prediction error is the difference between actual and predicted values.

Section C: Long Answer Questions ($5 \times 2 = 10$ Marks)

Q16. Explain Multiple Regression with equation.

Answer:

Multiple regression models the relationship between one dependent variable and multiple independent variables. The equation above shows how different factors contribute to prediction. Each coefficient (b_1, b_2, …) represents the influence of its variable.

For example, house price prediction may depend on size, location, and number of rooms. This approach gives more accurate predictions compared to simple linear regression.

Q17. Explain model evaluation in regression.

Answer:

Model evaluation in regression measures how well predictions match actual values. It uses error metrics like Mean Absolute Error (MAE) and Mean Squared Error (MSE). Lower error values indicate better model performance. Evaluation ensures reliability and accuracy of predictions.

Section D: Case Study (2 × 5 = 10 Marks)

Case:

A real estate company predicts house prices based on size, location, and number of rooms.

Q18. Which technique should be used?

Answer: Multiple Regression

Q19. Why is multiple regression suitable?

Answer:

Because multiple factors affect house prices.

Q20. What will be the output?

Answer: Continuous value (price prediction)

Q21. What is residual in this case?

Answer:

Difference between actual and predicted house price.

Q22. Why is evaluation important here?

Answer:

It ensures the model gives accurate price predictions.

Unit 12: Unsupervised Learning (Clustering – Advanced Concepts)

Includes complete answers (exam-ready format)

QUESTION PAPER

Time: 1.5 Hours

Maximum Marks: 30

Section A: Objective Type Questions ($1 \times 10 = 10$ Marks)

Q1. Unsupervised learning works on:

a) Labeled data

b) Unlabeled data

c) Sorted data

d) Cleaned data

Answer: b

Q2. Clustering is used for:

a) Prediction

b) Classification

c) Grouping similar data

d) Sorting

Answer: c

Q3. K-Means is a type of:

a) Regression

b) Classification

c) Clustering

d) Visualization

Answer: c

Q4. K in K-Means represents:

a) Data size

b) Number of clusters

c) Variables

d) Features

Answer: b

Q5. Centroid is:

a) Data point

b) Cluster center

c) Output value

d) Label

Answer: b

Q6. Clustering is based on:

a) Labels

b) Similarity

c) Random selection

d) Size

Answer: b

Q7. Which is an application of clustering?

a) Spam detection

b) Customer segmentation

c) Sorting

d) Printing

Answer: b

Q8. Outliers in clustering are:

a) Similar points

b) Extreme values

c) Labels

d) Features

Answer: b

Q9. K-Means algorithm updates:

a) Labels

b) Centroids

c) Data size

d) Variables

Answer: b

Q10. Clustering helps in:

a) Data deletion

b) Pattern discovery

c) Data storage

d) Printing

Answer: b

Section B: Short Answer Questions (2 × 5 = 10 Marks)

Q11. Define Unsupervised Learning.

Answer:

Unsupervised learning is a type of machine learning where models analyze unlabeled data to find patterns and relationships without predefined outputs.

Q12. What is Clustering?

Answer:

Clustering is a technique used to group similar data points based on their characteristics.

Q13. What is K-Means Algorithm?

Answer:

K-Means is a clustering algorithm that divides data into K groups by assigning data points to the nearest centroid and updating centroids iteratively.

Q14. What is a Centroid?

Answer:

A centroid is the center point of a cluster, representing the mean position of all points in that cluster.

Q15. What are Outliers?

Answer:

Outliers are data points that differ significantly from other data points and may affect clustering results.

Section C: Long Answer Questions ($5 \times 2 = 10$ Marks)

Q16. Explain the steps of K-Means clustering.

Answer:

K-Means clustering begins by selecting K initial centroids randomly. Each data point is assigned to the nearest centroid based on distance. Then, new centroids are calculated as the mean of assigned points. This process repeats until centroids no longer change significantly. It helps group similar data efficiently.

Q17. Explain advantages and limitations of clustering.

Answer:

Clustering helps identify patterns, group similar data, and support decision-making. It is useful in marketing and research. However, it requires choosing the correct number of clusters, is sensitive to outliers, and may not work well with complex datasets.

Section D: Case Study ($2 \times 5 = 10$ Marks)

Case:

A retail company wants to group customers based on purchase behavior to improve marketing strategies.

Q18. Which technique should be used?

Answer: Clustering

Q19. Which algorithm is suitable?

Answer: K-Means

Q20. What type of learning is this?

Answer: Unsupervised learning

Q21. What determines grouping of customers?

Answer:

Similarity in purchasing behavior

Q22. Why is clustering useful here?

Answer:

It helps in targeted marketing and better customer understanding.

Unit 13: Practical Work / Project (Data Handling & Analysis)

Includes complete answers (exam-ready format)

QUESTION PAPER

Time: 1.5 Hours

Maximum Marks: 30

Section A: Objective Type Questions ($1 \times 10 = 10$ Marks)

Q1. Practical work in Data Science focuses on:

a) Theory only

b) Hands-on learning

c) Memorization

d) Writing only

Answer: b

Q2. Data collection is the process of:

a) Deleting data

b) Gathering data

c) Sorting data

d) Printing data

Answer: b

Q3. Which tool is commonly used in practical work?

a) Paint

b) Excel

c) Notepad

d) Calculator

Answer: b

Q4. Data visualization is used to:

a) Store data

b) Represent data graphically

c) Delete data

d) Clean data

Answer: b

Q5. A project report includes:

a) Only conclusion

b) Only data

c) Complete analysis

d) Only charts

Answer: c

Q6. Data analysis helps in:

a) Ignoring data

b) Understanding patterns

c) Deleting data

d) Printing data

Answer: b

Q7. Which step comes first in project work?

a) Analysis

b) Problem identification

c) Visualization

d) Conclusion

Answer: b

Q8. Charts are used for:

a) Storage

b) Visualization

c) Deletion

d) Coding

Answer: b

Q9. Portfolio includes:

a) Only marks

b) Record of work

c) Only charts

d) Only theory

Answer: b

Q10. Viva voce evaluates:

a) Writing

b) Speaking and understanding

c) Drawing

d) Typing

Answer: b

Section B: Short Answer Questions (2 × 5 = 10 Marks)

Q11. What is Data Collection?

Answer:

Data collection is the process of gathering information from various sources for analysis and decision-making.

Q12. What is Data Analysis?

Answer:

Data analysis is the process of examining data to identify patterns, trends, and useful insights.

Q13. What is Data Visualization?

Answer:

Data visualization is the graphical representation of data using charts and graphs to make it easier to understand.

Q14. What is Project Work?

Answer:

Project work involves solving real-world problems using data science techniques such as data collection, analysis, and reporting.

Q15. What is Viva Voce?

Answer:

Viva voce is an oral examination where students explain their project and demonstrate their understanding.

Section C: Long Answer Questions (5 × 2 = 10 Marks)

Q16. Explain the steps involved in a Data Science project.

Answer:

A data science project begins with problem identification, where the objective is defined. Then data is collected from relevant sources. After that, data cleaning is performed to remove errors and inconsistencies. The next step is data analysis and visualization to identify patterns. Finally, results are interpreted and presented in a report with conclusions and recommendations.

Q17. Explain the importance of practical work in Data Science.

Answer:

Practical work is important because it helps students apply theoretical knowledge to real-world problems. It develops skills like data handling, analysis, and visualization. It also improves problem-solving ability and prepares students for real-life data science applications.

Section D: Case Study (2 × 5 = 10 Marks)

Case:

A student collects data on student performance and creates charts to analyze trends.

Q18. What is the first step in this project?

Answer: Problem identification

Q19. What is the process of gathering data called?

Answer: Data collection

Q20. Which tool can be used to create charts?

Answer: Excel

Q21. What does analysis help identify?

Answer: Patterns and trends

Q22. Why is report writing important?

Answer:

It helps present findings clearly and supports decision-making.

Unit 14: Project Work (Advanced – Data Analysis, Visualization & Reporting)

Includes complete answers (exam-ready format)

QUESTION PAPER

Time: 1.5 Hours

Maximum Marks: 30

Section A: Objective Type Questions (1 × 10 = 10 Marks)

Q1. Project work focuses on:

a) Theory only

b) Practical application

c) Memorization

d) Writing only

Answer: b

Q2. First step in a project is:

a) Visualization

b) Problem identification

c) Analysis

d) Reporting

Answer: b

Q3. Data collection involves:

a) Deleting data

b) Gathering data

c) Sorting data

d) Printing data

Answer: b

Q4. Data cleaning removes:

a) Useful data

b) Errors and duplicates

c) Charts

d) Graphs

Answer: b

Q5. Data visualization helps in:

a) Storage

b) Understanding data

c) Deletion

d) Coding

Answer: b

Q6. Which is used for data visualization?

a) Excel

b) Notepad

c) Paint

d) Calculator

Answer: a

Q7. Analysis helps in:

a) Ignoring data

b) Finding patterns

c) Deleting data

d) Printing data

Answer: b

Q8. A good report includes:

a) Only data

b) Only conclusion

c) Complete explanation

d) Only charts

Answer: c

Q9. Conclusion in project means:

a) Data collection

b) Final findings

c) Data cleaning

d) Visualization

Answer: b

Q10. Presentation skills are evaluated in:

a) Written exam

b) Viva voce

c) Practical file

d) Charts

Answer: b

Section B: Short Answer Questions ($2 \times 5 = 10$ Marks)

Q11. What is Project Work?

Answer:

Project work involves solving real-world problems using data science techniques such as data collection, analysis, and reporting.

Q12. What is Data Collection?

Answer:

Data collection is the process of gathering information from different sources for analysis.

Q13. What is Data Analysis?

Answer:

Data analysis is the process of examining data to identify patterns, trends, and useful insights.

Q14. What is Data Visualization?

Answer:

Data visualization is the graphical representation of data using charts and graphs.

Q15. What is Report Writing?

Answer:

Report writing is the process of presenting findings, analysis, and conclusions in a structured format.

Section C: Long Answer Questions (5 × 2 = 10 Marks)

Q16. Explain the complete process of a Data Science project.

Answer:

A data science project begins with problem identification, where the objective is defined. Next, data is collected from various sources. Then, data cleaning is performed to remove errors and missing values. After that, data analysis and visualization are carried out to identify patterns. Finally, results are presented in a report with conclusions and recommendations.

Q17. Explain the importance of data visualization and reporting.

Answer:

Data visualization helps simplify complex data using charts and graphs, making it easier to understand patterns and trends. Reporting presents findings clearly and supports decision-making. Together, they improve communication and help stakeholders understand results effectively.

Section D: Case Study (2 × 5 = 10 Marks)

Case:

A student performs a project on analyzing sales data and presents findings using charts and a written report.

Q18. What is the first step in this project?

Answer: Problem identification

Q19. What is the process of analyzing data called?

Answer: Data analysis

Q20. Which tool can be used for visualization?

Answer: Excel

Q21. What does visualization help identify?

Answer: Patterns and trends

Q22. Why is reporting important?

Answer:

It helps present results clearly and supports decision-making.

Unit 15: Viva Voce (Presentation & Conceptual Understanding)

Includes complete answers (exam-ready format)

QUESTION PAPER

Time: 1 Hour

Maximum Marks: 20

Section A: Objective Type Questions (1 × 5 = 5 Marks)

Q1. Viva voce is:

a) Written test

b) Oral examination

c) Practical file

d) Project report

Answer: b

Q2. Viva mainly evaluates:

a) Writing skills

b) Speaking and understanding

c) Drawing skills

d) Typing skills

Answer: b

Q3. Presentation skills include:

a) Only writing

b) Communication and explanation

c) Only charts

d) Only data

Answer: b

Q4. Confidence in viva helps to:

a) Reduce marks

b) Improve performance

c) Delay answers

d) Avoid questions

Answer: b

Q5. Clear explanation means:

a) Complex language

b) Simple and understandable answers

c) No answer

d) Long answers only

Answer: b

Section B: Short Answer Questions (2 × 5 = 10 Marks)

Q6. What is Viva Voce?

Answer:

Viva voce is an oral examination where students explain their project and answer questions to demonstrate their understanding of concepts.

Q7. Why is communication important in viva?

Answer:

Communication helps students clearly express their ideas, explain concepts, and answer questions effectively.

Q8. What are presentation skills?

Answer:

Presentation skills include the ability to explain ideas clearly, speak confidently, and use proper language and gestures.

Q9. How can a student prepare for viva?

Answer:

A student can prepare by revising concepts, practicing explanations, understanding project work, and improving communication skills.

Q10. What is confidence in viva?

Answer:

Confidence is the ability to answer questions without fear and present ideas clearly and effectively.

Section C: Long Answer Questions (5 × 1 = 5 Marks)

Q11. Explain the importance of viva voce in Data Science.

Answer:

Viva voce is important because it evaluates a student's understanding of concepts and practical work. It helps assess communication skills, confidence, and the ability to explain real-world applications. It ensures that students have genuinely understood their project work and can apply knowledge effectively.

Section D: Case-Based Questions (5 Marks)

Case:

A student presents a project confidently and explains all concepts clearly during viva.

Q12. What skill is demonstrated by the student?

Answer: Presentation and communication skills

Q13. Why is confidence important in this situation?

Answer:

Confidence helps in clear explanation and better performance.

Q14. What helps the student answer correctly?

Answer: Conceptual understanding

Q15. What is being evaluated here?

Answer: Viva voce performance

Q16. How can such performance be achieved?

Answer:

Through practice, preparation, and understanding concepts.

ADDITIONAL RESOURCES
ADDITIONAL RESOURCES

Videos

CLASS 10th Videos Playlist

Link:

https://www.youtube.com/playlist?list=PLzlh_31VWEFoVqTp4znpXOoWrT-cVwWMW

QR Code:

Exam Last Hour Review Questions Playlist Video

Link:

https://www.youtube.com/playlist?list=PLzlh_31VWEFrAuXqOQkh3-gvxGo1mf1m7

QR Code:

Annual Test Papers Exam Practises

Sample Paper I

Link: https://forms.office.com/r/rWMcnxW5PF

QR Code:

Sample Paper II

Link: https://forms.office.com/r/YQQdNbzfes

QR Code:

Sample Paper III

Link: https://forms.office.com/r/kCFQq40QRz

QR Code:

Sample Paper IV

Link: https://forms.office.com/r/JWwpZ29mZQ

QR Code:

Sample Paper V

Link: https://forms.office.com/r/uGuQtSnDqx

QR Code:

YouTube Videos Playlists for all Chapters

Chapter 1

Link:

https://www.youtube.com/playlist?list=PLzlh_31VWEFp4J4UOCFVbsIDPo0OsJNDX

QR Code:

Chapter 2

Link: https://www.youtube.com/playlist?list=PLzlh_31VWEFp8h4Q708212s_VJ6T1Z7p-

QR Code:

Chapter 3

Link: https://www.youtube.com/playlist?list=PLzlh_31VWEFrtqSK8wS3q9P46EdrhvuqS

QR Code:

Chapter 4

Link:

https://www.youtube.com/playlist?list=PLzlh_31VWEFpG3KKpNVamdN593C-jXaXy

QR Code:

Chapter 5

Link:

https://www.youtube.com/playlist?list=PLzlh_31VWEFqiNmnP8AB7vcoRgcNmTQpD

QR Code:

Chapter 6

Link: https://www.youtube.com/playlist?list=PLzlh_31VWEFrYIzRyJT3t1684R4Y6eLkm

QR Code:

Chapter 7

Link:

https://www.youtube.com/playlist?list=PLzlh_31VWEFp_wKlb9hGMAkkMDMxWOGpn

QR Code:

Chapter 8

Link: https://www.youtube.com/playlist?list=PLzlh_31VWEFr6v5XceXr3Een0UqYakky2

QR Code:

Chapter 9

Link: https://www.youtube.com/playlist?list=PLzlh_31VWEFpjV17QeFDfsqAeJXmeyV-5

QR Code:

Chapter 10

Link:

https://www.youtube.com/playlist?list=PLzlh_31VWEFpHkH8vfUXauLp_P0er8HN5

QR Code:

Chapter 11

Link:

https://www.youtube.com/playlist?list=PLzlh_31VWEFp764-2lTn-qRL_5mz5iwiD

QR Code:

Chapter 12

Link:

https://www.youtube.com/playlist?list=PLzlh_31VWEFoB4k8IomqfSy8KboMO03IW

QR Code:

Chapter 13

Link: https://www.youtube.com/playlist?list=PLzlh_31VWEFpb5S4aGdABgoQlv1cL0aXp

QR Code: